Also from Margaret Collins:

Because I'm Special
A Take-home Programme to Enhance Self-esteem in Children Aged 6-9
1 873 942 54 0

Circle Time for the Very Young
For Nursery, Reception and Key Stage 1 Children
1 873 942 53 2

Enhancing Circle Time for the Very Young
For Nursery, Reception and Key Stage 1 Children
1 904 315 17 8

Circling Round Citizenship
PSHE Activities for 4-8 Year-olds to use in Circle Time
1 873 942 59 1

Circling Safely
Keeping Safe Activities for Circle Time for 4 to 8 year olds
1 904 315 25 9

Just the Same on the Inside
Understanding diversity and supporting inclusion in Circle Time
1 904 315 56 9

But is it Bullying?
Teaching Positive Relationships to Young Children
1 904 315 43 7

Because We're Worth It!

Enhancing Self-esteem in Young Children

(Helping 4-9 year olds to feel good about themselves)

Illustrated by Philippa Drakeford

P·C·P

Paul Chapman
Publishing

ISBN 1 873 942 09 5

 Published by Lucky Duck
Paul Chapman Publishing
A SAGE Publications Company
1 Oliver's Yard
55 City Road
London EC1Y 1SP

SAGE Publications, Inc.
2455 Teller Road
Thousand Oaks, California 91320

SAGE Publications India Pvt Ltd
B-42, Panchsheel Enclave
Post Box 4109
New Delhi 110 017

www.luckyduck.co.uk

Printed in the UK by Antony Rowe Limited

Contents

Acknowledgements

My grateful thanks to

My grandchildren Amy, Harriet and Tom
who readily drew pictures to liven up this book.

Noreen Wetton
and other friends at the Health Education Unit,
Research and Graduate School of Education
University of Southampton, who are an inspiration.

George Robinson,
who edited sympathetically
with many useful ideas.

Introduction

It is not always easy to help young children to feel good about themselves. All too often they are told that they are not good, they are 'not old enough' they have done this or that wrong. How must it feel to be a young child at the mercy of all-powerful adults? Can you remember your feelings when, as a young child, you had made a mistake or did something wrong - and how daunting it was to face up to the 'giants' who had control over you?

If we want children to become positive members of society - to be able to learn and expect to succeed - we have to create the right climate for learning, give young children the chance to experience success without worrying that they are bound to fail and deal with any 'failures' in a sympathetic and understanding manner.

While creating a positive classroom environment with high expectations can increase children's self-esteem, it can also daunt those who know they can never come up to the standards required by the teacher. Do we sometimes forget to acknowledge human qualities as being as important as academic success - are only some qualities recognised, measured and rewarded?

Motivation - the challenge to succeed - is inbred in the human race. If success breeds success, what does failure breed? Many young children who experience frequent failure soon begin to doubt their own worth and expect to attain less. This breeds a reluctance to learn. Reluctant learners are evident ever earlier in our schools.

This book provides activities designed to help you to increase children's self-esteem and fulfill some expectations of the categories in 'Curriculum Guidance 5' - the document that set out, a few years ago, the nine aspects of health education that we should have been promoting with Key Stage 1 and 2. Why was the category about the psychological aspects of health education last in the list? Is this not one of the most important aspects of a healthy person?

Listed below are the skills and attitudes that most children 'could be expected to have acquired at the end of a key stage'. (Curriculum Guidance 5)

Key Stage 1 Psychological aspects of health education:
- understand the importance of valuing oneself and others
- begin to recognise the range of human emotions and ways to deal with these
- begin to be able to co-operate with others in work and play.

Key Stage 2 Psychological aspects of health education:
- recognise that individuals belong to many groups in which they will have different roles
- understand that individual responses to events will vary and respect other people's emotions and feelings
- understand that actions have consequences for oneself and others
- understand the meaning of friendship and loyalty and begin to develop skills needed to form relationships.

All the above skills depend on good self-esteem and good self-esteem depends on them. If we can develop these skills in KS1 and KS2 children, we go a long way towards giving them a firm foundation for their future adult lives as useful and fulfilled citizens.

A whole-school policy

Many school brochures or home-school agreements will have something written for parents about the importance of raising self-esteem of their children. This has to be taken on board by everyone who works in the school, not only teachers. Raising self-esteem among pupils will only work if all adults take care about the self-esteem of their colleagues. Children in schools see much more than we realise and will quickly tune in to a feeling of a lack of respect among adults - or lack of care about each other's feelings.

Many parents will be interested to know about this work you are doing in school and some could perhaps benefit by understanding the importance of self-esteem in bringing out the best in their children. Involve families by asking children to take some work home and ensure we are all working towards the same goals - building up self-esteem not breaking it down.

Page 148 of the National Curriculum Handbook (1999), gives a statement of values about 'the self' in which is stated the importance of 'valuing ourselves as unique human beings capable of spiritual, moral, intellectual and physical growth and development'. This book seeks to help teachers to deliver that part of the National Curriculum devoted to helping children to value themselves, to understand their own character, strengths and weaknesses and to use their talents and opportunities. By helping children to develop self-respect and self-discipline the children themselves can start to take responsibility for their lives. This will boost their self-esteem.

The National Curriculum Handbook, in its non-statutory guidelines for PSHE on page 136 suggest that activities and experiences across the curriculum will enable children to:
- recognise their own worth
- learn to co-operate
- become responsible for their own learning
- understand their personal and social development
- explore spiritual, moral, social and cultural issues
- respect common humanity diversity and difference
- recognise the importance of forming effective and fulfilling relationships so essential to life.

The activities in this book seek to help teachers to give practice in helping to achieve the above.

The National Curriculum states that teachers help children to:

- Develop relationships through work and play, e.g. by taking part in activities with groups that have particular needs, such as children with special needs and the elderly; communicating with children in other countries by computer links, e-mail or letters
- Take responsibility, e.g. for planning and looking after the school environment; for the needs of others, such as by acting as a peer supporter, as a befriender, or as a playground mediator for younger pupils; for looking after animals properly; for identifying safe, healthy and sustainable means of travel when planning their journey to school
- Feel positive about themselves, e.g. by producing personal diaries, profiles and portfolios of achievements; by having opportunities to show what they can do and how much responsibility they can take.

This book seeks to help to deliver this part of the National Curriculum.

What you get in this book

There are ten sets of activities, although activities in some of the sets overlap with complementing activities under different headings:

Loads of activities - Lots of things to do to raise self esteem!

What's your name?

Let's get to know who we are, get to know each other.

We're worth it!

Let's value ourselves, improve self-awareness.

Friendship

Let's think about what friendship means, how to be a good friend, to be loyal and true, our groups, our roles.

Body language

Let's explore senses, what our bodies can express, improve communication.

Intercommunication

Let's improve skills of listening, paying attention, improving expression, using imagination, avoiding conflict.

Explore feelings

Let's understand, express and manage our feelings, learn to understand/interpret others' feelings, how to deal with emotions.

Confidence building

Let's develop self-confidence, self-discipline, take responsibility, recognise our abilities, receive/give praise and encouragement.

Look at relationships

Let's consider others, feel safe, trust, appreciate/value difference, recognise and challenge stereotypes.

Empathy and sympathy

Let's put ourselves in someone else's place - feel their feelings with sympathy and recognise their needs.

Try, co-operate and succeed

Let's work together, share ideas, play our part, observe the rules.

Picture story books

Each set of activities has a list of suggested stories that can be used to link with the activities. You can use stories to help children to picture a situation in a way that is often not possible in other ways. If you stop reading occasionally and talk about how a situation is developing you will give opportunities for the children to relate the storyline to aspects of their personal and social development. Ask the children for their suggestions as to how the story might progress, such as:

- what might happen
- what they themselves would do in such a situation
- how the characters in the stories are feeling right now - or might feel if things don't change
- what they would tell the characters.

At the end of the story talk about how the character(s) resolved the situation and ask if they would have done it that way. Can they think of a different outcome?

These picture storybooks can be found in most schools, and at the time of writing, in all children's libraries. Some storybooks are integrated into an activity, others will support and enhance the activities in the section. Where a book is essential to an activity it is starred in the list - to give you time to locate the book in your school library or order it from the public library. Those unable to locate the actual book will find a synopsis of the story on page 105.

You will know other storybooks to add to the lists and can, on completion of each set of activities, ask the children to look in the libraries to see if they can find more picture storybooks on that theme. A space has been left under the list of books at the start of each set of activities for you to add others, helping you to build up a bank of appropriate stories for the future.

Let's celebrate!

Before leaving each set of activities it is suggested that the whole class engage in some celebration of what has been learnt and achieved. This could be a class celebration, a year celebration or a whole school celebration during which children from other classes could learn something of what has been learnt. Children could invite parents, families and other visitors to share in this celebration, thus opening up the learning to the whole community.

Each activity has the same format:
- a focus, linking it to the desirable outcomes of the National Curriculum
- the short activity itself
- development of the activity
- reflection, linking back to the focus of the activity.

You will find that you can use the activities in a very flexible way. They are suitable for even the youngest children in primary school. You will know the needs and abilities of your children and be able to choose appropriate work from each section - for example:

<u>Key Stage 1</u>

You may find that talking about the ideas in an activity is sufficient for the very youngest children, with only some being able to do the activity and without using the ideas in the Development at all. You could do this in Circle Time when the children are receptive to discussion. Then, in a further session, you might select an idea from the Development for discussion. Older Key Stage 1 children will be able to do the activities, but you may use the ideas from the Development to allow differentiation for more able children.

<u>Key Stage 2</u>

With older primary children, and depending on the stage of the children in your class, you might discuss the first activity as a starter and use mainly suggestions in Development. In a class with a wide range of abilities you can give different activities to various groups.

You can use the Activities and Development for the children to work as a class, in small groups, in pairs or individually. If you have assistants or trained parents/students you can enlist their help in working through some of the activities with small groups or individual children, especially if some of your children have special needs. If you work in this way you could select one Activity for a week, with groups of children (or individual children) working with the helper on different days, rounding up the week with a general discussion.

Children with special needs

Teachers of children with special needs or those working in special schools will find all the activities suitable for individual, group or small class work and very suitable for raising self-esteem of these sometimes vulnerable children.

How to use this book

There are always variations on how to use materials - you may wish to:

- dip in and select what is appropriate for your class
- select certain sections for a term's work
- use activities as a starter for more intensive work on that theme
- work through the book, using it as a long-term resource.

You may wish to use individual activities in response to the immediate needs of your children. In this case, select activities responding to that need, using the book as a resource. For example, if you have a child with disfigurement or disability, go to those activities that deal with this issue ('Someone Different' or 'Unkind Names').

You may wish to use each set of activities as a whole theme of work, before moving on to a different section, and if you choose this way of using the book, start by reading one of the stories, talking about the implications in the story and invite the children to select other stories that will fit in with the theme.

In order to really promote self-esteem it is important to highlight the children's achievements - however simple. You can do this by having a book of class achievements in which children can display their achievements, (from home and school) in pictures or writing. Or you may prefer each child to have their own book of personal achievement (see activity "How well do I know myself") for them to include in it a description of all the things they do well. You may need to help under-achievers to find something they are good at doing to include - all children have some talents - even if it is for washing the paintbrushes well or organising/tidying class displays.

If you have a reward system in operation you could ensure that children include these rewarded activities in the record.

Circle Time

If you use Circle Time as part of your day or week you will find that most of these activities will work easily in Circle Time, where you have a close group of children ready to listen together and ready to obey your Circle Time rules.

If you are using the first part of the activities as a 'starter' you will find that a close knit group is almost essential to allow for the rapport that you will generate and to enable the children to respond easily.

There are several ideas for organising Circle Time for children of different ages and stages in *Circle Time for the Very Young* Collins, M. (2001).

The ten sections

What's your name?
Sing your name
Sharing names
Greetings
Unkind names
Nothing
Let's celebrate

We're worth it
Feeling good
Things I like to do
I don't like
How well do I know myself?
We are all stars
Let's celebrate

Friendship
Mrs Spoon's Family
Good friends
I value my friends
Friends in different networks
Falling out of friends
Let's celebrate

Body language
Let's move
Be still
Calm down
What do I mean?
Words help
Let's celebrate

Intercommunication
Are you listening?
Stop and listen
Back and forth
Don't shout about it!
Keep in touch
Let's celebrate

Explore feelings
What Makes Me Happy
I whistle a happy tune
How do you feel?
How am I feeling?
Help me to tell you
Let's celebrate

Confidence building

Amazing Grace
I like me
I can do it
At school I'm really good at…
How do you feel about it?
Let's celebrate

Look at relationships

What I like best about you is…
Caring
I'd like to be…
Underneath the surface
Someone different
Be careful not to bully
Let's celebrate

Empathy and sympathy

Harry's shoes
Someone different
Jojo overdoes it
Dan all alone
Just as you are
Let's celebrate!

Try, co-operate and succeed

Our responsibilities
Rules are OK!
I know I should but…
Let's find out together
Classroom values

Let's Celebrate!

I'm feeling good already!

What's your name?

Let's get to know who we are, get to know each other.

Setting the scene for these activities

In this set of activities the aim is to help the children to understand that names are really important. They establish our identity; they tell people who we are and help us to know who other people are.

Encourage children to use people's names as often as possible. Make sure you don't refer to people by their job title - the caretaker, secretary or dinner lady; use people's names and ensure that the children do. When children know and use people's names it gives them self-confidence in dealing with people; this raises self-esteem.

A good start to the day when checking which children are present in class (during registration) is to say "Good morning" to each child, using their name and making eye contact. Expect each child to return the greeting, using your name and with eye contact. You may like to allow a few moments for the children to greet their friends in the same way.

There are many children's picture books that use unusual names for people, toys or animals. You might like to share some of the following with the children:

Nothing, Mick Inkpen, Hodder
Rumpelstiltskin, Helen Cresswell, Macdonald
Wilfred Gordon McDonald Partridge, Mem Fox, Penguin
Izzy and Skunk, Marie-Louise Fitzpatrick, David & Charles Children's Books
Omnibomulator, Dick King-Smith, Young Corgi

The five activities in this section

Sing your name helps children to learn the names of others and to reinforce their memory of their names in a fun way. As a starter to the activities in this section it sets the scene for recognising the importance of using people's names. It is more suitable at the beginning of a school year. You can expand this activity by asking children to use percussion to beat out the rhythm of their name or to add a statement to sing - I am May Jones and I like fish.

Sharing names helps children to know that though there may be other with the same name, our names are still our own possession. The children are asked to think about how family names (surnames) came about and how these are passed down through families. Older children could use library books to find out about surnames or ask their families if they know the origin of their own surname.

Greetings helps children to think of ways of greeting people they know and the importance of saying good morning to people they meet each day. Children are helped to think about how to greet people new to them in a way that will make them feel comfortable. Suggestions are given to practising shaking hands - a skill that young children often find difficult. You could also introduce children to the 'grand chain' used in country dancing. (Children stand in a circle, number 1, 2 around the circle and ask ones to face twos. Each child puts out their right hand and grasps the right hand of the person facing them. They walk past that person, and hold out their left hand to the next person and continue around the circle.)

Unkind names reminds children that name-calling can be hurtful and that it is important to respect people's names and use them correctly. Using nicknames can be hurtful - unless the person chooses their own nickname. You might like children to think up a nickname they would like to have and ask them to tell or write about why they would choose this name.

* Nothing emphasises our need for names so that we can embrace our own identity. If you cannot locate this picture storybook you can use the synopsis on page 105, and you will need to engage the children in discussion about how a person might feel if they had no name. You could ask the children to write a story about a character called "Somebody" and ask how they think a person would feel if people said they were 'really somebody'

Sing your name

Focus

To help children to get to know names of others in the group in a fun way and to learn that names are important as they are our own, usually unique, identity tag.

I am Dermot Cunliffe
and I like to play football

Activity

Tell the children that names are very important - names tell people who we are and we have to try to remember to use people's names. Tell them that they are all going to sing their names and can use any tune.

Start with your name, sing it twice - make it tuneful and as long as possible. "Mi-sses Ba-rring-ton, Mi-sses Ba-rring-ton". Ask the children in turn to think of a different tune and sing their names - using all their first names.

Explain that their parents were very particular about choosing names for them when they were babies because they know that names belong to children for the rest of their lives. Ask the children if they have seen any of the books that are produced for parents to help them to choose names for their babies.

Development

Ask children to add a short sentence about themselves - also singing - allow children to 'pass' if they wish. Ask the children if they know anyone else with the same name as theirs - if so how do they feel about that?

Ask the children to draw a picture of themselves, to write their name and something about them. Ask older children to work in pairs to find out about (and write down) how some first names came about and their derivatives - e.g. Margaret, Marguerite, Daisy, Rita. They could write a poem about names they like.

Reflection

Remind the children that it is important to use people's names when you are talking to them - our names are our own personal tag and belong to us.

Sharing names

Focus

To help children to know names of others in the class, apart from their own friends, and to give the opportunity of using both their names which (usually) makes each child unique.

This is my family

Our family name is Cooper. Mum is Mrs Cooper and I am Lisa Cooper and my brother is Harry Cooper. I have a Granny Cooper. A 'cooper' is someone who mends casks or barrels.

Activity

The teacher will know all the children's names and may have several with the same first name. Ask all the children named "xxx" to stand up and sit down quickly. Do this several times to include those who share names and those who do not. You may have some with the same surname. You may have some names that rhyme - e.g. John, Ron and Don, Jill and Bill, Mick and Dick. Ask children to do some activity when you say the initial sound of their name e.g. tap your nose/pat your head, if your name begins with the 'sh' sound.

Development

Talk with the children about the family names we have that are shared with members of our extended family - aunts, grandparents etc. Can the children think of how some of these family names came about? Explain that in Britain our family names have been family names for generations and that many people with the same surname may have been related to each other a very long time ago.

Ask the children to draw some of the people in their family with the same family name and to write about these people.

In Spain a man and women keep their names when they marry and the children have part of their mother's surname name and part of their father's. Can the children find out about customs of names in other countries and cultures?

Sensitivity warning - *omit this activity if there is a child in the class who could be upset by this. You could, instead, ask the children to draw the people who live in their house and write their names alongside their pictures.*

Reflection

Remind the children that we are all unique but have similarities with other people.

Greetings

Focus

To introduce and practise greeting someone new to the class in a way that will make them feel comfortable and welcome.

Activity

Tell the children that people new to the class, whether children or grown-ups, can feel uncomfortable, shy or worried and that we have to make them feel welcome and part of the class.

Ask children, in turn, to take on the role of a new pupil and introduce the routine with "Today we have a new child coming to join our class (or school). I'm going to ask him/her to introduce him/herself." The children can use their own name or make one up.

The 'new child' says, for example:

"I'm Jamail Tandy and I'd like you to call me Jimmy."

The class responds with,

"Welcome to our class Jimmy."

We think a new person might feel:

shy

worried

anxious   lonely

uncertain

we would try to help them to feel better in our class.

Development

Repeat the game with other children representing other newcomers - a new teacher, classroom helper, mid-day assistant, caretaker or visitor. Ask the children to think of how they would feel if they were new to the class - collect the words they tell you and make a list that can be used in the children's writing.

Explain that adults often greet each other by shaking hands or kissing and that different countries have different ways of greeting people. Show children how to shake hands correctly - using their right hands.

Play a 'shaking hands' game by asking the children to walk, skip or run about the room, stopping on a command and shaking hands with the nearest person. (Teachers could greet children by shaking hands with them once a week.)

Ask older children to find out ways to address royalty, religious leaders or judges when speaking or writing to them. Ask them to write a speech, with the correct opening address.

Reflection

Remind the children that people's names are very important to them. It is also important to know how to address people. To make people feel good about being with us we need to pronounce their names properly and call them by the name they prefer. Talk about how hurtful it is for people to have their names mispronounced or not used.

Unkind names

Focus

To help the children to remember that it can be hurtful and unkind to misuse people's names or call them nicknames they don't like.

Activity

Tell the children this story of Jamie.

Jamie had always had a red birthmark on his neck. When he was little he didn't know about this, but when he went to playschool someone called him "Redneck" and other children joined in. Jamie was so upset that he didn't want to go to school for a long time. He always wore a high necked jumper and never wanted to take it off when he was doing PE.

We like to be called these names..

kind careful

tidy friendly

clever good

Ask the children to think of how Jamie felt when people called him that name.

Ask the children to close their eyes and think of something they don't like about themselves. Ask them to open their eyes and think how they would feel if someone called them a name that showed they knew this.

Now ask the children to think of something about themselves they feel good about - something they would like to be called. Help children to understand what you mean by saying something about yourself - e.g. "I wouldn't mind if people called me helpful."

Collect the children's responses.

Development

Now, go through the alphabet asking children to think of words beginning with 'a' that they would like to be called - e.g. active, able, angel, artist, athlete, awake. You may need to pass with some difficult letters!

Ask older children to think of (and write down) ten or more words beginning with different letters of the alphabet that they would like to be called, and put these words in alphabetical order. They could use dictionaries to help them.

I would like to be called:

angelic
beautiful
clever
daring
excitable
friendly

Reflection

Remind the children about unkind name-calling and how unpleasant this can be. Help them to feel good about finding words that describe their own good qualities and those of other people.

* Nothing

Focus

To reinforce the need to use people's proper names and to think of the feelings of people who lack self-esteem.

Activity

Read the book *Nothing* by Mike Inkpen (or use the synopsis on page 105). Ask the children to tell you how they think that Nothing felt, squashed in the dark attic at the start of the story, when it could not remember who it was. Ask them how they think Nothing might have felt when it heard someone say - "Oh it's nothing".

Nothing

felt sad
was lonely
had no-one
was lost
cried
didn't know his name.

Did the children think that Nothing was male or female?

The story says, "How do you think you would feel if you had been squashed in the dark for years and years. And then you squeezed through a tiny hole to find yourself under the big starry sky?"

Ask the children to tell you words to describe the feeling.

Ask the children to draw Nothing as it looked when it was left all alone in the house and to write down how Nothing felt.

Can the children remember the sequence of the story - how Nothing remembered it used to have ears, whiskers, tail, stripes? How do they think Nothing felt at the end of the story when he had a real name that told everyone he was Toby. How do they think Little Toby felt when he was in the cot with the new baby?

Development

Talk about how Nothing felt when he didn't have a name - he felt worthless and useless. Ask the children to tell you why they think we have names and why it is important to use people's names. Ask them how they feel when people they don't know well have remembered their names.

Ask them to draw a picture of themselves and to write their name and why they think it is important to have and use people's names.

Reflection

Remind the children to use people's names when talking to them. Explain that it is not unkind to ask someone's name if you do not know it or if you have forgotten it. Remind them that your name is your own identity tag - it helps other people to remember who we are. Tell the children to make sure they use other people's names correctly and with respect.

My name is Rashid and I am a boy. I think we have names because it helps people to know who we are and it tells people if we are a boy or a girl. We know people are talking to us when they use our name and we have something to write on our work to show it is ours.

My name tells you...
  I AM ME

Let's celebrate!

On completion of these activities, encourage children to evaluate their own learning by looking at what they thought or knew before doing the activities. Make sure that the children realise that they have been learning about the importance of people's names and the need to use them correctly.

Talk about or ask them to write down what they think they have learned while doing this work.

Ask the children to make a poster to recognise that names are important.

Ask them to design a certificate to award themselves for their good work.

Make a wall display to show the importance of using people's names.

We're worth it!

Let's value ourselves, improve self-awareness.

Setting the scene for these activities

Here we are focusing on the good qualities the children have. You may need to point these out to some children. It is essential to focus on positive qualities that we all have - the capacity for love, our health and strength, our feelings of kindness, trying hard, being on time, putting things away, considering others, being friendly, cheerful, helpful. By actively focusing on the children's good qualities - and letting others see that you value them, you will be raising self-esteem of the members of your class.

Make sure you remember to do this with the adult members of your class too - the children will pick up on your comments which will strengthen their own sense of belonging to a worth while class.

There are many children's picture books with storylines that illustrate people feeling good about themselves. Here are just a few you might like to share with the children:

Ruby, Maggie Glen, Red Fox
Mary Mary, Sarah Hayes & Helen Craig, Walker
Piece of Cake, Jill Murphy, Walker
What Makes Me Happy? Catherine & Laurence Anholt, Walker
Badger's Bad Mood, Hiawyn Oram & Susan Varley, Picture Lions

The five activities in this section

Feeling good
The whole essence of self-esteem is to feel good about yourself. Here children are asked to think of the things that make them feel good, why these things make them feel good and how exactly they feel inside. They are asked to share these feelings with the rest of the class. Talk with the children about where in their bodies they feel these good feelings. Do all children feel them in the same place?

Things I like to do
Children may need help to realise that they don't all have to like doing the same things. Most children prefer to conform and feel comfortable when they are similar to their peers. They may need to be encouraged to explore their individuality while at the same time respecting the right of other people to be different and to prefer doing different things. Extend this activity by asking children to do a survey of what adults (home or school) like to do in their spare time.

I don't like
This activity will help children to realise that people are allowed to 'not like' certain things, as long as they then allow others to have this same choice. Children may need help to realise they should be tactful about not insisting on their own way and be prepared to go along with the majority choice. Follow up the activity by talking about what adults do when there is a difference of opinion - how do they find out and abide with the majority opinion?

How well do I know myself?
Children may need help in exploring their own personal abilities and the things they want to improve about themselves. They may need help in identifying the things they can do well, could do better and need to make a real effort to improve. You could ask each child or each group to identify something they would like to improve, to set themselves a target and monitor their progress.

We are all stars
This helps the children to focus on their good qualities and abilities, reinforcing their self-esteem and allowing them to openly celebrate and feel proud of these. Extend this activity by asking children to focus on a member of their family and identifying one or more things that the person does really well.

Feeling good

This makes me feel good.

I feel good when my Mum reads
me a story before I go to bed.
I feel warm inside me.

Focus

To help the children to focus on things that make them feel good and think about how this makes them feel inside.

Activity

Ask the children to draw a picture of themselves doing something that makes them feel good. Ask them to label their picture, write what they are doing, or dictate to you so that you can write for them.

Development

Ask the children to share their picture with a friend, and talk about what they are doing and why this makes them feel good. How did it make them feel inside?

In each class group ask each child to tell you what they drew that made them feel good. Discuss the kinds of things they drew - are many of them similar things? - are some of them unusual? - do other children like doing those things? Come together as a class and ask children who are willing to share their work. Can they think of ways to help other people to feel good - especially people who are different in some way?

Reflection

Remind the children that we are all different and we all have different ways of feeling good. Explain that it is important to feel good about ourselves. When we feel good in ourselves we find things easy and are good to be with.

Things I like to do

Focus

To help children recognise that we all like doing different things and that this is OK.

Activity

Ask the children to think of something they like to do at school. Start them off by telling them your name and what you like - e.g. "I am Mr Tims and I like telling you a story." Try to include all children to at least say their name but allow them to 'pass' if necessary. Ask children to draw themselves doing something they enjoy doing.

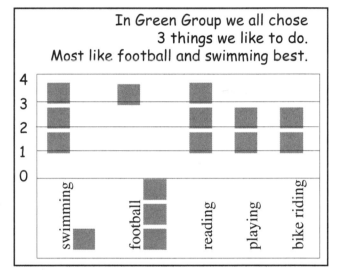

In Green Group we all chose 3 things we like to do. Most like football and swimming best.

Development

Ask the children to think of things they like to do out of school. Ask them to quickly draw or write down one thing they like to do. Make a list of those things on the chalkboard so the children can see them. Look at the list and decide which is the most popular activity, the least popular.

Working in groups ask the children in each group to make a list of things they like to do - each child can add no more than four things to the list. Then ask each group to display their data in some way.

(E.g. they could draw a group picture, make a pictogram, each child draw one activity and write how many children chose that one, use the computer to generate a graph.)

Reflection

At the end of the session come together as a group and ask the children to help you to remember what all the children said so that they can see that many of us like to do different things. Remind the children that just as we are all different, so we all like to do different things. Recognising that we all like to do different things, while respecting the right of other people's preferences, enhances our self-esteem.

I don't like...

I don't like walking to school in the rain.

Focus

To help children to recognise that it's OK not to like some things.

Activity

This is a negative version of the previous activity. Ask the children to think about the things they don't like to do at home. You can start by saying your name and what you don't like - e.g. "My name is Miss Bloggs and I don't like washing up."

Development

Ask children to think of something else they don't like to do out of school. Ask for volunteers to stand and mime what s/he doesn't like to do. Accept only 2 guesses before asking the child to tell what they were miming, so that a lot of children have a turn. Before completing the session ask children to tell you all the things that have been mentioned by others as things they don't like to do at home. Are there similarities/differences? Could the children record this in some way?

(If you want to include all children over a period of time ask each 'mimer' to write what they mimed on a list with their name.)

Reflection

Remind the children that just as we all like to do different things, so we all like not to do certain things. Remembering this will help us to understand that our friends may like to do different things and that sometimes we go along with other peoples choices in order to be fair. Respecting other people's right to choice while preserving our right to prefer something different can make us feel good about ourselves.

How well do I know myself?

Focus

To help children to recognise and value their personal abilities, while recognising things they would like to improve about themselves.

Activity

Tell the children that you wonder if they know you. Tell them a few of your personal abilities and ask them if they knew this. Say, for example that:

- you try hard but find it impossible to get round to talk to them each day
- you enjoy planning work for them
- you find it almost impossible to hear them read as much as you would like.

Tell the children that you are going to help them to find out about themselves. Ask them to help - say:

- touch your head if you think you are kind to animals
- smile widely if you think you are a good friend
- touch your shoulders if you think you are helpful to people
- fold your arms if you try to think about other people's feelings
- touch your nose if you always try to be fair to others
- touch your ears if you find it easy to play with anyone.

You could add to this list some qualities you think the children could improve - listening skills, waiting, taking turns, sharing.

Development

Write down some of these abilities (skills) on the board and ask the children to draw themselves putting into practice the things they find easiest and hardest to do. You could make a display of the children's work, surrounded by the qualities you explored, or ask the children what they think they are all good at, as a class and display this with positive messages.

In our class we are all very good at listening to stories. We always sit quietly and listen.

Ask children to record their own achievements in a personal diary or folder. Start this off by helping them to make and decorate a folder or a cover for their diary and writing in a list of their own achievements to date. Ask them to write down at the back of the folder two or three things they would like to improve about themselves - they can mark these in some way every time they make progress there.

Encourage the children to update their diary every week or so.

Reflection

Remind the children that they all have lots of good personal qualities and they should remember these when things go wrong and they feel bad. There will be things they would like to do better and individually they can work towards this. Remind them that as a class they are good at certain things - help them to be proud of the things they do well and proud of being in your class.

We are all stars

Focus

To help children to value their good qualities and to reinforce their feelings of self-worth.

Activity

Ask the children to think of all the things they are good at.
Give ideas such as helping, sharing, painting, reading, playing, listening, being happy.

Ask them to close their eyes and think of as many things as they can.
Ask children to:

- touch their ears if they can think of three or more things they are good at
- touch their head if they can think of two things they are good at
- touch their shoulders if they can think of one thing they are good at.

Ask each child to finish the sentence: "I am good at…"
Allow children to pass, but go back to them at the end.

Development

Tell the children that they are going to make a sky full of stars. Ask a group of children to make a sky background and ask the rest to draw and cut out a large star. (You may need to make a template for very young children.)

Ask the children to draw themselves on their star doing one thing that they are good at and to write what this thing is. Some stars can be glued on to the sky - hang others to dangle. Ask the children to think of a good title for this display - e.g. We are all stars. Ask children to add speech bubbles/notices to tell others how this display came about - what they had to do and how important it is to recognise the things we are good at being or doing.

Reflection

Remind the children that we are all good at doing something, and better at doing some things than at doing others. When we feel sad that we can't do something we must remind ourselves that we can't all be good at everything and remember the things we can do well.

Let's celebrate!

On completion of these activities, don't forget to encourage children to evaluate their own learning by looking at what they thought or knew before doing the activities.

Remind the children they have been thinking about their own self-worth. Display their stars where the rest of the school can see them and ask children to draw and write about the work they have been doing to add to this display. You could display some of the books you and they have read underneath the display, with appropriate quotations. Add some relevant questions so that other children can interact with the display. Questions such as:

How many stars are about school?

How many stars are about things children do outside school?

What would you write on a star about yourself?

What would you like to be able to write on a star about your personal qualities?

You could put paper and pencil near the display and a box or large envelope for the children's answers.

Friendship

**Let's think about what friendship means, how to be a good friend,
to be loyal and true, our groups, our roles.**

Setting the scene for these activities

Here the focus is on what good friends are and do and that there are friends for different activities. The children are asked to identify family friends, neighbourhood friends, friends of different ages and in various networks.

Children are asked to think about the qualities they look for in their friends and the qualities they themselves need if they are to be a good friend.

There are many children's picture books about friends, some with storylines that tell about the value of friendship. Here are some you might like to share with the children:

Mrs Spoon's Family, Malorie Blackman, Andersen Press
Orlando's Little While Friends, A Wood, Child's Play
Oscar Got the Blame, Tony Ross, Beaver
My Great Grandpa, Martin Waddell,
Walker
I Love You Blue Kangaroo, E.C.Clark,
Andersen, London,
Little Beaver and the Echo, Amy
MacDonald, Walker Books, London

The five activities in this section

*Mrs Spoon's Family

If you don't have access to this book, read and use the synopsis on page 105. This activity helps the children to focus on loyalty to friends and to be aware of the need to be watchful that other people don't spoil their friendships. It also touches on jealousy - the animals next door being jealous of the contentment of Mrs Spoon's family. Extend this activity by talking about when the children themselves have felt jealous about something or someone - try to help them to see that jealousy is non-productive and is a feeling we must try to recognise and control.

Good friends

This activity helps the children to think of the qualities we need to have in order to be a good friend. They are helped to explore the nature of friendship as a sharing of friends without jealousy and without putting yourself first. Talk about adult friendships that have stood the test of time - people who have had a partnership that has lasted - e.g. Morecambe & Wise.

I value my friends

Children will have different friends in different areas of their life. Some will be adult friends; some may be pets. All friends need to know they are valued and children may need help either in putting this into words or acting in such a way as to show they value friends. Extend this by talking about how being selfish has no place in true friendship - are they able to put their friend first?

Friends in different networks

This activity helps children to look at the friends they have for different occasions. They may need help in understanding that a 'best' friend in one network may have other 'best' friends in other networks and that sharing friends is the best way of having friends.

Falling out of friends

Children fall in and out of friends easily and part of growing up is knowing the importance of making up with people with whom we have had a disagreement. It is not easy to say 'sorry'. This activity gives children the opportunity to practise saying sorry by acting a part. Help the children to realise that it is not weak to be the first to say 'sorry' and that it's not a case of 'giving in' but rather that it takes strength to be the first to make up.

* Mrs Spoon's Family

Focus

To help children become aware of how important friendship is - and to be strong and loyal to their friends and family.

Activity

Read *Mrs Spoon's Family* to the children and talk about how Cat and Dog felt - at the beginning of the story, in the middle and at the end.

Ask the children to tell you words to describe how Mrs Spoon felt at the end of the story. Make a list of these words on the chalkboard or flip-chart and ask the children to write down these words in some order - alphabetically, in order of depth of feeling. (If the children have dictionaries or wordbooks they can keep these words there.)

Development

Working in groups ask the children to choose one part of the story to illustrate as a group picture. Ask the children to write an appropriate sentence underneath, making sure they use at least two of the words from the list.

In movement, ask the children to work in pairs and be Dog or Cat and show how they felt in various parts of the story. They could then work in threes - with Mrs Spoon - and act out the story with imaginary cats and dogs off stage.

Reflection

Remind the children the importance of keeping their friendships safe and how to deal with people who try to spoil friendships. Remind them that they can listen to criticism about friends but that they have to make up their own mind whether this is true or not.

40

Good friends

Focus

To help children to focus on friendships, what you need to be and do to be a good friend and what to expect from friends.

Activity

Ask the children to tell you what they think a good friend is and does and collect the words they give you on a flip-chart.

Ask the children to work in pairs to draw a picture of good friends and to tell each other how they have shown that this is a picture of a good friend.

Ask the children to work in their working groups and show and talk about their pictures. Can they identify and write down two or three things they think are important in a friend? Ask them to choose one person from their group to tell everyone their list.

Talk about qualities you wouldn't want in a friend - for instance, jealousy and possessiveness - and the importance of sharing friends.

Friend words
caring   helping
thinking of you
playing together
liking each other
wanting to please
letting others join in
taking turns
sharing things.

Development

Ask the children to compose a word portrait, song or poem about being a good friend - they can use some of the 'friend' words to help them do this and choose their own title.

Reflection

Remind the children that these words they have used about a good friend are qualities that are very important in forming friendships. If they themselves want to be a good friend they will need these qualities in themselves. Having friends and being a good friend is important - help children to recognise that some people have lots of friends and others have only one or two and that the number of friends you have doesn't matter.

I value my friends

Focus

To help children to understand the importance of showing that they value their friends and that in so doing, they themselves will be a valued friend.

Activity

Tell the children that you have to work at being a good friend. You have to show your friends that you like them and want to please them. Ask them what they can to do show this.

Ask them to think of what they have done today to show their friends that they really value (care about) their friendship.

Ask them to:

- raise one hand if they have played with a friend today
- clap once if they have shared something with a friend
- lift their elbows if they have done something to help a friend today
- nod their head if they have listened to a friend today
- close their eyes if they have talked to a friend today.

You can share things with them.
You can play with them.
You can think of their feelings.
You can listen to them.
You can tell them your problems.
You can trust them.

Development

Ask the children to think back to what they wrote in the earlier activity 'Good Friends'. Did they include pets as friends? Talk about other friends - grown-up friends, friends in their family, their neighbourhood, in a group to which they belong or a pet that is a friend.

Ask the children to draw one of these friends and to write about the friendship. Ask the children to find books about different kinds of friends to add to your list.

Reflection

Remind the children that they have friends of different ages and in different circles. Explain that it is just as important to show they care for these friends as well as friends of their own age at school.

Friends in different networks

Focus

To help children to recognise that they will have different friends in different networks and that we have to share our friends.

Activity

Ask the children to think of and tell you all the different groups that they are a part of. Collect their responses in a list.

Ask the children to indicate who belongs to each group and note the number alongside.

Talk with the children about the different friendships they have within these networks. Do some friends appear in several networks? How do they feel about close friends who don't belong to some networks? It would be appropriate to read the story of *Orlando's Little While Friends* alongside this activity.

Development

Organise, label and display large pieces of paper for several networks. Ask the children to draw pictures of themselves in the networks to which they belong. They can do this directly onto the paper, or by using separate paper and sticking their picture on. Ask children to write about their friends in one network and add this writing to the display. Older children might consider other networks of people who might need friends - people in groups that have particular needs - old people, people who are ill or live alone, people with language difficulties or physical needs.

Reflection

Remind the children that it is OK to have different friends for different occasions, but that they can belong to networks without having a special friend there. Explain that if their special friend doesn't belong to a particular network they can cultivate other friends. We can't own friends - good friends know it is important to share friends.

Falling in and out of friends

Focus

To help children recognise that we have times when we fall out of friends with people, but that we can find ways to make up these friendships.

Activity

Tell the children the story of Sam and Chris (who can be boys or girls).

Sam and Chris were two good friends who always played together. One day they had a quarrel and Sam said s/he would never play with Chris again.

Ask the children to suggest what Sam actually said.

Ask them to suggest what Chris replied.

Sam went to one part of the playground and Chris went to the other.

Ask the children to show by their faces and body language how Sam and Chris were feeling.

Then it was time to go into the classroom and both children went to their work places.

Divide the class into their working groups or groups of around six/eight children. Ask half the groups to think of and discuss ideas of what Sam could do to make up, while the others talk about what Chris could do. Use a timer to allow only five minutes for this.

Call the children together; ask each group to tell the other groups their suggestions for making up. Would any of their suggestions work?

With the class all sitting, ask children who thought about Chris to stand up and find a partner sitting down (who thought about Sam), and work in pairs, one taking the role of Chris, the other Sam. Ask them to take turns in saying sorry.

Sam and Chris - Saying Sorry is not easy.

They both felt sad and wanted to make up but didn't know what to do. Then Sam went to Chris and said "I'm sorry, let's be friends again." and Chris smiled and said "Yes, let's, I'm sorry too."

Development

Ask the children to work in pairs and make a picture of Sam and Chris, and to finish the story telling what Sam and Chris said and did to make up again. What will they call their picture? Can they write a message or a good rule to help people who fall out of friends to make up?

Reflection

Remind the children that there will be times when they don't agree with their friends and sometimes they may 'fall out'; that you don't have to agree with your friends all the time but you don't need to stop being friends just because you don't agree with them over some issues. We all need to remember that there are ways to make up and that someone has to be the first to say 'sorry'.

Let's celebrate!

On completion of these activities, don't forget to encourage children to evaluate their own learning by looking at what they thought or knew before doing the activities.

You could:

- Make a large 'Friendship' display to share with the school and include pieces of work from the five activities, especially work about saying sorry.
- Choose one of the storybooks to illustrate with pictures and captions telling the story
- Ask the children to write a letter to a friend telling their friend why the friendship is important to them
- Make a class 'Friendship Book' with contributions from all the children about friends outside school
- Act out the story of Sam and Chris as part of an assembly - or to children from other classes
- Divide the class into four groups, each to peer teach another class about their work on friendship
- Invite a seeing or hearing dog with its owner to come to talk to the children in the classroom
- Contact another school with a view to exchanging friendships by visit, post, email, fax or computer links.

This is Max.
He is a seeing dog.
Max brought Mrs Green, who is blind, to school to visit us. She told us all the things Max does to help her.

Body Language

Let's explore senses, what our body language can express, improve communication.

Setting the scene for these activities

Here the focus is on face and body language - how you can read people's feelings from their expression and posture. Children are encouraged to relax and move in ways that show expression of feelings. It is important for children to be aware of how people are feeling, not only by the words they use but by reading their manner through observation. When children can read face and body language they will find it easier to relate to others and this will reinforce their own self-esteem.

Many children's picture books show, (either in the storyline or in the illustrations) with face and body language, how people are feeling. You might like to share some of these with the children:

What Makes Me Happy, Catherine and Laurence Anholt, Walker
Nancy No-Size, by Mary Hoffman and J. Northway, Methuen Children's Books
What Else Can You Co?, Jean Marzollo and Jerry Pinkney, Bodley Head
The Boy on the Beach, Niki Daly; Bloomsbury Publishing
Sing to the Stars, Mary B. Barrett, Little, Brown & Co.

The five activities in this section

Let's move

A physical activity which helps the children first to focus on different ways of moving, then to consider facial expression as a language. Body movement can help us to recognise people we know well and facial expression can show our true feelings. You could follow up this activity by asking children to report on what they did and how they felt during the session.

Be still

A practical activity during which children think of ways to relax and calm down if they feel anxious or threatened. They explore various attitudes and think of words to describe their feelings. You could collect the words they give, ask the children to group them in some way and display them as useful vocabulary.

Calm down

This activity asks children to think of when they feel most calm and then to make a calming mind picture to call upon when they feel anxious or unsure. To reinforce this picture the children are asked to draw what they have visualised. Music can have a calming influence; you could listen with children to quiet music such as the Andantino from Mozart's Flute and Harp Concerto, Delibe's Flower Duet, Satie's Gymnopedie No 1 or Howard Blake's Walking in the Air, all on "The Best Classical Album in the world…ever." (EMI). Can they themselves compose quiet music? Colour evokes moods and this is also explored. You might like to use Murray White's CD *Picture This* - Guided Imagery for Circle Time.

What do I mean?

A practical session where children are asked to communicate without words and to respond to each other. Some children are fairly good at reading adult body language but find it less easy to read their peers' body language and to communicate to them in this way. Talk about when we have to rely on reading body language - when communicating with people with hearing difficulties or when in a foreign country and ask for children's experiences of these.

Words help

Another way of helping children to look at body language using the children's own postures and then drawings. To further explore this you could ask the children to bring in to school photographs or pictures cut from magazines that show how people are feeling by their body position or facial expression.

Let's move

Focus

To help children relax and enjoy moving in different ways.

Activity

Tell the children that they are going to move in different ways around the space you have and that they must not bump into anybody or anything.

Now suggest that they move first like a kitten then like an old cat. Can they feel the difference?

Can they move like a snake and then like a cheetah? - Like a new baby and then like an old person?

Development

Use percussion to help the movements to flow. Ask one half of the class (in secret) to move in the manner of someone sad while the other half try to guess. Change over. Then choose other feelings - such as angry, excited, happy, scared etc.

Tell the children that sometimes people can recognise us, even from a long distance by the way we move - can they think of people they would easily recognise? Can they tell you what it is about these people that makes them easily recognisable?

Reflection

Remind the children that people can often recognise how others are feeling by their facial expression and the way they sit, stand and move. If they want to feel good about themselves they can project a good image of themselves to others by acting and moving in a positive way.

I can always tell when it's my Dad – he moves from side to side when he walks.

Be still

Tense is
tight, stiff, hard,
spiky, jerky.

Relaxed is soft,
smooth, light,
slow, gentle.

Focus

To help children to relax and feel themselves relaxed. This will help them if they feel anxious, unsure or afraid.

Activity

This activity is suitable for a PE or movement time as it needs space.

Ask the children to:

- lie on the floor and make themselves feel as heavy as they can
- slowly lift one arm as though it were a heavy weight - allow it to fall, do the same with the other arm
- lift one leg - allow it to fall - then the other leg
- tighten up their shoulders - then relax them
- tighten up their neck - then relax
- breathe slowly and deeply.

Add other tense and relaxing movements as appropriate - e.g. faces, eyes, tummies. Explain that relaxation with slow deep breathing is a good way to help you to control yourself if you feel tense, angry, worried or anxious. Counting to ten is another way to regain self control.

Development

Ask children to move around the space in a relaxed and floppy way, then tense up on a command - clapped hands, drum roll etc. Ask them to move in various attitudes - angrily, frightened, unsure etc. and after each attitude to relax completely and take deep breaths.

Can the children think of words to describe how they feel when they are tense and when they are relaxed? Can they describe how they feel when they are in and out of control?

Reflection

Explain that there is time to be active and a time to be relaxed. Remind children that sometimes it is inappropriate to move and act quickly. They need to move more slowly and gently when near babies, shy animals, timid people etc. Remind the children that relaxing and taking a deep breath is a good way of controlling feelings. To feel good about ourselves we need to be in control of our feelings.

Calm down

Focus

To help the children to focus on ways of calming themselves down if they get too lively or upset.

We feel calm...
before going to sleep,
when we wake up,
when we have a cuddle,
when watching
something quiet on TV,
when painting or drawing.

Activity

Remind the children how they learned to be tense and relax. Ask them to tell you when they feel the most relaxed and calm.

Ask the children to sit quietly, legs crossed, hands on knees with their eyes closed for 30 seconds and to make a picture inside their heads of something beautiful or comfortable.

Ask the children to stretch, stand slowly, stretch again then sit down again.

Ask children to tell you about the picture they made in their heads. Could they remember and hold on to this picture when they feel angry or upset? Ask them to try to remember how they felt looking at the picture they made inside their head.

At the end of the session ask the children to draw the picture of something beautiful or comfortable they pictured. Ask them to tell you about it or write a few lines describing it.

Development

Talk about how different kinds of music can evoke various moods. Select some tapes or CDs that produce a feeling of calm in you and listen to some pieces with the children. Can children think of any particular music or song that makes them feel calm and happy?

Ask the children, working in pairs or small groups, to select some percussion instruments and compose some calming music. Allow each group to demonstrate their music to the class if they wish. Talk about colours and ask the children to paint using the music you chose as stimulation, using only a few (perhaps three) colours of their choice.

Reflection

Remind children that we all get tense or uptight at times and that we need a technique to help us to relax. Explain that when we relax our body language slows down and helps us to cope with whatever is making us feel tense. Tell children that it is a good idea to relax and count to ten before reacting to something upsetting. Staying in control of our feelings makes us feel good about ourselves and confident in what we are doing.

What do I mean?

Focus

To help the children to understand non-verbal communication and body language.

This is a picture of Jane and me. We had to use our body language to talk.

Activity

Tell the children that you are going to talk to each other without using words. Demonstrate this by choosing a partner and use gestures and touch to persuade them to accompany you to a different part of the room (beckon to them, take their hand and smile etc.). Use gestures to persuade them to sit beside you (beckon to them and pat a chair or the floor beside you).

Ask the children to work in pairs, label them A and B and ask the As to persuade the Bs to sit down, stand up, go away, etc. then change places.

Ask the As to show anger, happiness, fear and other feelings with the Bs responding to that body and facial language. Change over.

Allow children to practise and then ask each half of the class in turn to watch the other half.

Ask the children to work in pairs, with one person 'talking' without words. (e.g. miming eating an ice cream or reading a book) and the other person trying to guess. Change over after each mime.

Development

Ask children if they can show a negative response to the person doing the persuading. Again you may have to demonstrate with a partner - trying to persuade them to sit, stand, relax, while your partner resists your suggestion. Ask the children whether they found this easy - or not so easy.

Ask older children to record this exercise in picture and writing.

Reflection

Remind the children that it is important to look at people's body language if you are to understand how they are feeling. Remind them that other people will know how they are feeling by watching how they move and it is not always necessary to use words at all.

Words help

Focus

To help the children to use vocabulary to interpret body language.

Activity

This is excitement. It is hard to draw it.

Tell the children that you are going to show with your body language what you are feeling, and ask them to write down a word or two to describe what they think you are feeling.

First choose an angry posture, give the children a minute to write down what they think, and then write up 'angry'. Ask the children to raise a hand if they wrote 'angry' on their paper.

Do this with other postures - e.g. happy, worried, bad-tempered etc. and after each, tell the children what you were trying to portray and ask how many could read your face and body language. You can make a game of this and ask a children to take your place whispering to you what they are trying to convey.

Explain that it is not always easy to correctly read body posture and that words can help a lot.

Development

For younger children collect magazine pictures of people's faces which show different feelings/emotions, such as anger, pride, happiness. Ask the children to tell you what feelings are showing on the faces. Do they all agree?

Ask older children to draw pictures of people in various attitudes - showing anger, happiness, worry, fear, etc. Ask them to write the attitude on the back of their picture. Spread some of these on tables and ask children to guess what attitude is supposedly portrayed, before asking them to turn over the picture to check what is intended. Change over the pictures and give everyone a chance to guess some of them. The children will find this difficult - without words to help it is not easy to interpret moods.

Talk with the children about the difficulty of reading face and body language and help them to understand that it is necessary to talk about how you feel, especially if you are worried or unsure.

Reflection

Remind the children that it can be easy to misinterpret face and body language -especially if there are no words to accompany it. Some people always look happy and people thinking about something else can often look stern. Face and body language only gives clues to how people are feeling and we must talk about how we feel about things so that people will get the right message.

Let's celebrate!

On completion of these activities, don't forget to encourage children to evaluate their own learning by looking at what they thought or knew before doing the activities.

Use some of the children's work to make a final display about body language. Ask the children to add to this by writing about how different pieces of music make them feel. Add the pictures they painted using music as a stimulation.

If you can, invite a musician or music specialist into school to talk to the children about how they use music to evoke moods.

Perhaps you could visit an art gallery or exhibition of paintings to try to define the mood the artist is trying to create. Otherwise use reproductions of paintings in books to do this in the classroom.

Is there a deaf person you could invite into school who could talk to the children about how they manage to communicate without words - do they use sign language or lip-read?

Mr Forster

Mr Forster is deaf and he has to try very hard to talk to people. He has a hearing aid but sometimes this doesn't work in a noisy room. He has to watch your face all the time so that he can understand what you are saying.

Mr Forster is deaf but he doesn't like people shouting at him. He can read your lips.

Intercommunication

Let's improve skills of listening, paying attention, improving expression, using imagination, avoiding conflict as well as those of speaking and writing.

Setting the scene for these activities

Children who feel good about themselves and have high self-esteem usually have good communication skills. We can help them to understand the importance of really listening and understanding what is meant by what is said. In this world of TV with visual information, children often do not pay sufficient attention and only receive part of a verbal message. When listening, the hearer has to show that s/he is really listening. When talking, the talker may need to emphasise the message by using repetition and different vocabulary.

You may like to share the following books with the children:
The Nature of the Beast, Jan Carr, Tambourine
Mrs Gaddy and the Ghost, Wilson Gage, Bodley Head
Don't Forget to Write, M. Selway, Red Fox
Why Is The Sky Blue, Sally Grindley & S. Varley, Andersen Press

The five activities in this section

Are you listening?

A practical activity to help the children realise the difference between hearing and listening. The teacher models good listening skills - showing concentration, using eye contact and paying attention by nodding or smiling. Then the teacher models poor listening skills, by looking all around, fidgeting and obviously not paying attention.

Stop and listen

A practical listening activity where children have to concentrate on the sounds around them. You could use various areas of the school and surroundings for this - library, corridor outside the hall, near a class doing PE. There are educational sound tapes that would be useful for this kind of activity [such as 'Soundtracks', from Living and Learning (Cambridge) Ltd 1993] or you could make a tape using sounds indoors, outdoors and from TV.

Back and forth

An activity to help children appreciate how in conversation the talk goes back and forth between the speakers. Young children may need quite a bit of practice with this activity before going on to do it without your prompt sound. Extend this with older children by asking them to work in threes or larger groups and then discuss how large groups (meetings/parliament) have a method of allowing people to speak. The main point is to help children to realise that if people speak at the same time, nobody gets heard.

Don't shout about it!

A discussion activity to help children explore the various kinds of communication and ways of dealing with shouting. Explain that speaking quietly can be more effective in communication than shouting, although clarity is important. You could play "Chinese Whispers" to illustrate this! (Sitting in a circle the first child whispers something to the second child who then repeats it to the next child until the last child hears the message and speaks it out aloud. The first person then tells what the original message was.)

Keep in touch

The children look at various methods of communication and when these are appropriate. The children could keep a record of what they have been doing - a log or diary of how they organised their work and what worked or didn't work.

Are you listening?

Focus

To help children to practise listening skills and really hearing what is said.

Activity

Talk with the children about the importance of showing that we are listening. Ask them how they can do this.

Ask the children to work with a partner - one to be the talker and the other the listener. Give the children a starter for talking and listening. This could be:

'A time when I felt disappointed/happy/sad/scared was...'

Encourage the listeners to show that they are listening and understanding what the person is saying.

Warn the children when it is nearly time to stop - allow only 30 seconds for the youngest reception children and up to a minute or even two for older juniors. Ask for listener volunteers to tell the class what they have been listening to, then check with the talker that this is correct. Reverse roles and change the topic.

Development

Ask children to demonstrate with face and body language:
- someone who is really listening and understanding
- someone who is half listening and waiting to interrupt
- someone who is not listening at all, but thinking of something else.

Emphasise the importance of eye contact.

Ask the children to work in pairs to draw a picture of two people talking together and try to show that the listener is really listening. The children can use speech bubbles or write a sentence that shows that the listener is really listening.

Reflection

Remind the children that listening is a skill which makes the speaker and the listener feel good. Ask them to say how they could tell that the listener was really listening.

Stop and listen

Focus

To help the children develop more acute listening skills.

Activity

Tell the children that it is important to really listen hard if they want to hear all that is going on around them. Ask them to sit still and close their eyes and listen for 30 seconds or one minute and try to guess and remember every sound they hear. (You may like to make some sounds if you are in a particularly quiet area.)

We went on a listening walk.
I heard...

someone coughing,
the copying machine.
a bird, a car.

I didn't hear..
the door close
the wind in the trees.

Ask the children to open their eyes and tell you what they heard. You could ask children to write the sound they heard on a flip-chart/chalkboard as others tell what they heard.

At the end of the session look at the list and see if any of the sounds can be grouped together - several bird songs, traffic, coughing. Link with colour any sounds that are the same in some way.

Development

Take the children for a listening walk around the school or outside in the grounds to listen to the sounds there. At various points stop all movement and listen for 30 seconds or more. You may like children to have a paper and pencil so that the can record the sounds they hear. Once back in the classroom collect the sounds and try to group them as before. Talk about the sounds they heard - did all children hear the same sounds? Did some miss some of the sounds? Why? Ask children to record what they did during the walk and the sounds they heard.

Ask children to think about people who are blind and how they have to rely on their listening skills. Talk about hearing dogs for people who cannot hear. Explain that it is important to respect the feelings of people who do not have all the five senses and make sure we try to communicate in a way which is helpful.

Reflection

Remind the children that really listening is an important skill. People who listen to instructions or for information find that it is easy to get on with their work. People who don't listen carefully often misunderstand - and then feel silly or unhappy when they do the wrong thing.

Back and forth

Focus

To help children to communicate in a better way, by learning the art of conversation.

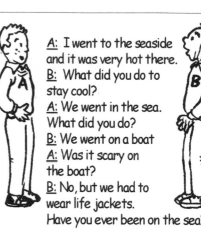

A: I went to the seaside and it was very hot there.
B: What did you do to stay cool?
A: We went in the sea. What did you do?
B: We went on a boat
A: Was it scary on the boat?
B: No, but we had to wear life jackets. Have you ever been on the sea?

Activity

Explain that both talking and listening are very important in their friendships. Tell them that it is difficult to listen if you are trying to say something, and it is difficult to talk if you are listening to something or someone else. Explain that conversation is like a game of tennis - one person hits the ball (talks) then the other person returns the ball (the talk) back. Asking a question about what the first person said is a good way to show you are listening.

Ask the group to work in pairs and set a subject for their talk - e.g. holidays. Tell the children that you are going to allow one of each pair to talk first with no interruptions from their partner. On your signal (clap or percussion bang) the talker must finish their sentence. Then tell the listener it is their turn to talk - to reply to the first person's talk, ask a question or say something relevant to what s/he has been listening to. Then the second person can tell something of their own. Repeat this a couple of times, using your signal to help the children to practise sharing the talking and listening.

Once the children have understood the activity, repeat it without the change over signal. After a couple of minutes sit down together to discuss the activity. Ask children to touch their elbows if they managed to bat the conversation back and forth, to wriggle a thumb if they forgot to answer the first person's talk and to touch their nose if they found it easy.

Development

Ask children in pairs to write down a conversation between two people showing that the talk is going from person to person. Show them how to write down the talk.

Reflection

Explain that it is not easy to listen carefully to other people when you have something important to tell. Remind them that it is important to listen to others, to respond to what you hear and to wait your turn to talk. Sharing a conversation fairly isn't easy, but it comes with practice and will help you to feel more confident about yourself.

Don't shout about it!

People talk in many ways

* quietly
* shout
* scream
* move a lot
* look people in the eye
* look away from people
* get hot and bothered.

Focus

To help children to think of various ways to avoid verbal conflict.

Activity

Tell the children that there are lots of different kinds of ways of talking to people. Ask the children to tell you some. Ask the children what they could do when children get angry and shout at them. Collect their suggestions and talk about the best things to do.

Development

Ask the children to think of a time when they got angry with someone and think of what they did. Was it a good thing to do? Did it help? Could they have done something better?

Ask the children to work in pairs with one person acting 'getting angry' and the other practising what to do. What works best?

Ask the children to write down what seems to work for them.

Reflection

Remind the children that we all get angry at times and that it's OK to let the anger out as long as we don't take it out on someone else. Explain that it is sometimes important to get angry - when thing happen that we know are wrong. It is important is to not let the anger get the better of you. Remind children to think carefully what to say - and how to say it - so that they help to make things better. Ask them to try to remember this when they get angry or when other people get angry with them.

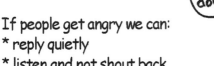

If people get angry we can:
* reply quietly
* listen and not shout back
* say 'calm down, I'm listening'
* walk away
* look them in the eyes
* make ourselves tall and stand firm.

Keep in touch

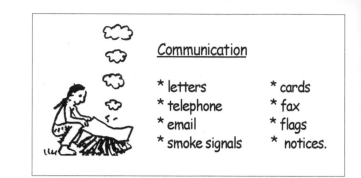

Communication

* letters   * cards
* telephone   * fax
* email   * flags
* smoke signals * notices.

Focus

To help the children to use various means of communication; to plan and evaluate the organisation of their work.

Activity

Ask the children to describe different ways of communicating with people as well as talking and listening. Make a list of these. Explore with the children these various methods of communication and consider when they are appropriate.

Ask the children to work in groups to find out about one of these methods. Ask them to plan how they are going to do this and to show you this plan before they start work.

In a whole class talk about the children's work and how they set about it. Did their planning work? Would they do it differently another time? How have they recorded their work? Was it appropriate?

Development

As the groups of children finish their work, ask them to decide how best to display their findings for everybody to understand what they have been doing and what they discovered. They could for example, make group books, class or group displays, individual or paired records, display their data using the computer or make pictograms.

Talk with the children about communicating with children in other countries - by email, fax or letter. Can they develop links with another school - perhaps even an EEC school where children speak English? Is there a local group that would benefit from having a link with the children in your class - e.g. children with special needs, a community group such as 'Age Concern' or a charity such as 'Save the Children'.

Reflection

Remind the children that they have been discovering various ways of communication and that they have been in charge of their own learning by finding out and making decisions about how to pass on what they have learned. Explain that working in this ways helps them to feel good (confident) about the work they are doing and shows how capable they are.

Let's celebrate!

On completion of these activities, don't forget to encourage children to evaluate their own learning by looking at what they thought or knew before doing the activities.

This set of activities would lend itself as a basis for a class assembly. Collect pieces of work the children have been doing on intercommunication and ask them to illustrate each of the five sections by painting or drawing themselves doing the work, which they can then present to their year group or school. You might like to add work about how people communicate in certain situations:

- when meeting important people
- when in various locations - hospitals, libraries, fairgrounds, swimming pools
- when doing various activities - playing tennis, swimming, birdwatching, fishing.

Find out about the origins of old forms of communication - semaphore, Morse, telegram, cables, telex, ship's flags

Interest children in more modern forms of communication - Braille, signing for deaf, digital, satellite, computer link-ups. Can they find out how they work?

Find out more about the people who invented the communication aids listed above, and about how the telephone cables were installed under the sea.

Could some children invent their own systems or signs - danger signs, flags,

Perhaps children could design a picture postcard warning about the danger of too much sun on holiday.

I have been learning about flags.
A flag can be called a standard or a banner.
A flag of distress is either at half-mast or flown upside down.
A flag of convenience is a flag of a country flown when merchant ships are owned and registered by other countries to avoid taxes.
A flag of truce is usually a white flag carried by someone to show they come in peace.
A flag day is a day when money is collected for charity.
The Queen's flag is called the Royal Standard and shows when she is there.
Our flag is the Union Jack and is three flags in one.
The pirate's flag is the Jolly Roger.

Explore feelings

Let's understand, express and manage our feelings, learn to understand/interpret others' feelings, how to deal with emotions.

Setting the scene for these activities

Children who are confident and have high self-esteem are usually good at interpreting other people's feelings and sharing their own. Many children will need help to recognise various feelings and vocabulary to express them.

When choosing stories to support this theme look for those which portray different feelings or show an understanding of feelings or a change in attitude at the end of the book. You may like to share these with the children:

Sheila Rae, The Brave Kevin Henkes, Picture Puffins
What Makes Me Happy Catherine and Laurence Anholt, Walker
Piece of Cake Jill Murphy, Walker
Two Monsters David McKee, Beaver
Daisy Rabbit's Tree House Penny Dale, Walker

The five activities in this section

* What Makes Me Happy

The picture book of this title is most appropriate for this activity, as it shows faces expressing so many different emotions (synopsis on page 105.) If you can't locate it use pictures collected from magazines or newspapers, (ask the children to bring some in before you start). Alternatively you may have other books to hand with pictures showing various facial expressions that you could use.

I whistle a happy tune

This activity is dependent on you having the music or knowing the words to the song. Most public libraries have cassettes to lend. If you are unable to get a recording you can talk with the children about the things people are afraid of and how they overcome their fears.

How do you feel?

It is important that children learn to read people's expressions and after following the suggestions in the activity you could make a fun game of making statements with completely the wrong facial expression - for instance saying you are very pleased with a deep frown on your face, or saying you are cross with a wide smile. Children could play with this idea in pairs before coming together to discuss their feelings at these conflicting signals.

How am I feeling?

Children need to widen their language of feelings and this activity can help. You can also extend this vocabulary by displaying a list of 'feelings' words with plenty of room for children to add to them as they/you come across them in your reading.

Help me to tell you

The aim of this activity is to help children to realise that it is good for us to talk about our feelings. They will need a good vocabulary of feelings words in order to do this. You could reinforce this message by talking about misunderstandings that can occur when people do not clearly say what they mean and when those listening do not probe to make sure they are hearing what the talker means to say.

* What makes me happy

Focus

To help children to focus on various feelings.

Activity

Read the picture book *What Makes Me Happy?* to the children - first straight through and then go through it a page at a time sharing the pictures. As you do this, ask the children to try to make their face show the feeling on each page.

Talk about all the emotions shown in the book and how they were portrayed.

Write up the feelings on a chalkboard and ask the children if they can suggest others to add to the list.

Development

Read through the list of feelings and ask children to work in their groups to choose one of these feelings and make a whole group picture to show this. Ask the children to add writing to their picture to make it clear what the feeling is and how they have illustrated it. Ask them to write an explanation of how they decided which feeling to choose and how they planned their work.

Reflection

Remind the children that we all have feelings such as those shown in the book - some are good feelings we feel glad about but some are scary or sad feelings and we need to share these with someone we trust.

Tiger group all wanted to chose to illustrate 'scared'.

We drew lots of scary things -
monsters,
bangs,
high walls,
witches,
sharks,
dark places,
worries.

We all did one scary thing, cut them out and overlapped them to make the picture. Sally arranged them best so we let her.

I whistle a happy tune

Focus

To help children realise that we are all afraid of something and that we have to find ways of dealing with this fear.

> When people are afraid, they can...
> * remember it is not real
> * talk about it
> * keep away from it
> * think of ways to deal with it
> * take care when around it.

Activity

Use the song "I whistle a happy tune" from "The King and I" . Listen to the song first and hear the words. In movement ask the children to put actions to the song, stopping the music from time to time to share how various children have interpreted the words.

Sit down and talk about the things that people are afraid of. Make a list of these and talk about each one in turn.

Finish the session by acting out the song once again.

Development

Go through the words of the song once again. Talk about the words "no one will suspect I'm afraid" and ask the children if they think it is a good idea to pretend they are not really afraid. What else could they do? Do they think it a good idea to talk to someone they trust about their fears?

Ask the children to help you to make a list of the things people could do to help them to cope with their fears. Ask them to make their own list of people they can tell about things that make them afraid.

Reflection

Remind the children that most people have something they are afraid of and it's not a good idea for young children to try to overcome them without help. It can help a lot to talk about things to someone they can trust and to let that person help them to overcome their fears.

How do you feel?

Focus

To help children to read and interpret other people's expressions and to understand how their expression shows how they are feeling.

Activity

Ask the children sit in a circle or loose group so that they can easily see each other. Start by making your face show some kind of expression of emotion and tell the children how you feel e.g. "I feel very tired".

Ask the children to make a tired kind of face and repeat the sentence. Choose several children to stand up and show the class the expression on their 'tired' face.

Repeat the activity with other emotions.

Development

Develop this activity by asking children to volunteer to show some expression of feeling and asking the rest of the class to guess what it is. You can make this fun by giving (or writing up) two or three examples of what the expression might be and asking the class (or individual groups) to guess which they think it is.

Ask older children to work in their groups to record what they have been doing. Ask each group to make a plan first with details of what they will need to carry out their plan.

Expressions.

We made a zig zag book with 5 pages - one each and we decided which expression we would record.
Jan drew the best picture.
He drew George's face showing horror - but nobody could guess it.

Reflection

Remind the children that they have been learning to look at people's faces to read their feelings. Tell them that it is helpful to know how people are feeling or how they are reacting just by looking at their expression. It helps people to feel confident and they relate to people better if they can recognise how others are feeling.

How am I feeling?

Focus

To help children to increase their language of feelings.

Activity

Ask the children to sit in a circle or loose group so that they can easily see each other. Tell the children that they are going to think of why today they feel as they do. Start by saying "I'm feeling good today because…" finishing the sentence with a reason.

Go around the circle/group, asking the first children to end the sentence in their own way. Change the feeling after a few children have responded by using other feelings, e.g. hot, sad, excited, jolly, restless, hungry. (Make a personal note of the feelings words you use.)

Development

Ask children to work in their groups and quickly make a list of as many of the feelings words they can remember. Come together as a class and ask the groups how many words they remembered. Did any group remember them all?

Make a full list of all the words and ask the children to copy these words into their wordbooks. Ask children to think of a time when someone they knew had one of these feelings. Ask them to illustrate and write about the occasion.

How am I feeling?

hungry, thirsty, cold, too hot, uncomfortable, tired, friendly, confident, upset, excited, listless.

Reflection

Remind the children that they have been learning new words to convey their feelings. Tell them that they need to learn new words so that they can understand more exactly what other people mean and tell others what they themselves mean. It helps people to feel confident if they have a good vocabulary to use when talking or writing.

Help me to tell you

Focus

To help children know they need to tell people their feelings and to extend vocabulary of feelings.

Activity

Tell the children this story.

Nabrana was ill in hospital and couldn't talk because of a very, very bad sore throat. Bill went to see him and took a present. Nabrana wanted

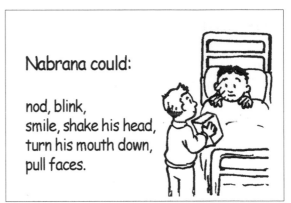

Nabrana could:

nod, blink,
smile, shake his head,
turn his mouth down,
pull faces.

to talk but couldn't say a word. He could only look. Bill said he knew Nabrana wanted to say 'thank you' for the present. Bill wanted to know how Nabrana was feeling and when he would be able to play again.

Ask the children to tell you what Nabrana could do to 'talk' to Bill without words.

Development

Ask the children to tell you how they think that Nabrana was feeling. Make a list of the words they use. Help the children to extend their vocabulary by asking for alternatives to some of their words and give examples when their contributions dry up. It would be a useful aid to creative writing to have a list of these words on display.

Ask the children to work in pairs to decide what they would do if they suddenly found they were with an alien who couldn't talk their language. Ask them to write down what they would do, how they would feel, how the alien would feel.

You could further develop this activity by talking about how people who are blind, deaf or can't speak manage to communicate (see ideas on page 53 - celebrating body language).

Reflection

Remind the children that we sometimes need to help people to tell us of their feelings and it is important to know the right words to use. Caring people will always take time to listen carefully and try to understand what people are meaning to say.

Let's celebrate!

On completion of these activities, don't forget to encourage children to evaluate their own learning by looking at what they thought or knew before doing the activities.

This set of activities could celebrated by following up the alien idea in "Help me to tell you". Tell the children that these aliens are made from metal and have no feelings - they live by strict mechanical rules. Tell the children that a family of them came to earth and wanted to know about all the feelings that humans have.

The children could make a whole family of aliens to display, initially with writing about where they came from and their lives on their own planet. Ask each pair of children to choose one of the feelings they have talked about during the activities and to write an explanation of it, giving examples of what people say and do when they feel this way.

Ideally this display should be in a communal area of the school so that other people can read and share in the explanations.

You could ask the youngest children to help you to write a class poem - perhaps starting each alternate line with "When I feel... I..." or using colour to describe feelings. Older children could write poems about their feelings on special occasions - such as starting a new class/school, moving house, buying new clothes, going on holiday, having someone to stay.

Feelings by Henry Ellis

When I feel happy,
I have a big smile.
When I feel sad,
my mouth goes down
When I feel excited,
I jump for joy
When I feel lonely
I want to cry.

Coloured Feelings by Josie Crabtree

Red is the colour of my anger
Blue is when I feel calm
Green and I'm not nice to know.
Purple is when I'm angry and grim
Black, when I'm hateful and horrid
Orange is when I feel happy and bright
And yellow is when I feel on top
of the world.

Confidence building

Let's develop self-confidence, self-discipline, take responsibility, recognise our abilities, receive/give praise and encouragement.

Setting the scene for these activities

Some children need help to increase their self-confidence - especially those who are not good at classwork. These activities give children the opportunity to look at what they are good at and to recognise and value their achievements.

Fostering self-confidence in children helps them to feel good about themselves, thus raising their self-esteem.

Choose books where children or animals gain in confidence as the story progresses. Books such as:

* *Amazing Grace* Mary Hoffman, Frances Lincoln

Mary Mary Sarah Hayes & Helen Craig, Walker

Badger's Bring-Something Party Hiawyn Oram & Susan Varley, Andersen

Windhover Alan Brown & Christian Birmingham, Collins

I know what I am good at... swimming.

The five activities in this section

*Amazing Grace
This activity relies heavily on the storybook - if you can't get it use the synopsis on page 105. You could use another book that tells of someone who achieves something through determination and practice. Extend the activity by talking about how we have to work at most things if we want to succeed. Ask children to identify things they want to do/be when they are older and talk about how they might achieve this.

I like me
Tell the children that we all need to like ourselves deep down even if we fall short of our own expectations at times. This activity helps children to focus on the things about themselves that they feel good about. You can extend this by asking them to look at positive qualities in others - perhaps characters in books you have read together. Ask them to try to identify what it is about these characters that they like and whether they would like these qualities in themselves.

I can do it
This activity focuses on the learning process, the need to practise and not be discouraged. Extend the activity by talking about successful people they know - artists, musicians, sportspeople talk about how these people have got where they are - what they had to do in order to be successful, what they had to sacrifice. Ask the children to identify a new skill to learn or improve now - perhaps catching/ bouncing a ball or skipping; they will need to record present ability, set a target, practise and record progress.

At school I'm really good at…
This activity helps children to focus on their abilities. You may need to help some of the less able children to think of the many things they can do - such as helping, listening, drawing, running, clearing up, caring, keeping things tidy. Help children to add to their list of three things they are good at doing each time they have a small success. Review your class 'reward system' and see if it can be extended to help low achievers to record success.

How do you feel about it?
In this activity we help children to identify when they have been successful. Many children only know they have done well when we praise them. How do they feel then? Ask them where they feel these feelings of wellbeing - on their face, in their head, heart, stomach - does it make them feel tall? Extend this activity by talking with children about the times when they have done something well and no-one knows about it. Can any of them think of times when this has happened? How do they feel then? Does it make them feel less good about it?

*Amazing Grace

I am trying to learn to skip. I have to practise

Focus

To help children to recognise that if they really want to do something enough they can find a way, but you have to persevere and keep trying.

Activity

Read the story of *Amazing Grace*.

Ask the children to tell you how they think Grace felt when:

- she was told she couldn't be Peter Pan because she was a girl
- she was told she couldn't be Peter Pan because she was black
- she went to see the ballet
- all the children voted for her
- the play was over.

> Grace was:
> hard-working
> thoughtful
> kept trying
> didn't give up
> determined.

Development

Ask the children why they think the children in the story voted for Grace. Did Grace herself do something to help to get the part - or was it just luck? Ask the children to think of some words to describe the kind of person Grace was.

Ask the children to draw a picture of Grace and write a sentence about the kind of person she was.

Reflection

Remind the children that we can't expect luck to help us to do things. We have to work hard and keep trying. It isn't always easy, but if we always do our best we can achieve most things we want to do. Explain that when people are successful at one thing they begin to feel more self-confident about other things.

I like me

I'm Luigi and I like having brown eyes and black hair.

Focus

To help children to think about themselves and something about themselves that they like.

Activity

Tell the children that everyone has something about themselves that they like - and don't like. Ask the children to think of something about themselves that they like. Start by saying your name and saying something about yourself that you like - e.g. "I'm Mrs Green and I like being tall". Ask the children in turn to say their name and something about themselves that they like. Children can pass if they have nothing to say - you can ask them at the end if they have thought of something. Children may repeat what another child has said and this is acceptable.

Development

Tell the children about something that you yourself enjoy doing and can do well. If necessary explain the word 'confidence'.

Ask the children to draw or paint a picture of themselves being confident and doing something they can do well. Ask them to write a speech bubble telling how they feel when they are doing this. Make a display of all the pictures with the speech bubbles to share with the rest of the year or school. Ask the children to think of a title. You might use this as your theme for a class assembly or encourage some of your class to tell other children about making the display and the things they feel confident about.

Reflection

Remind the children that no-one likes every single thing about themselves- they cannot change the way they look, for example. Thinking about what they like about themselves can change the way they think about themselves.

Remind the children that they can feel rightly proud about the things they can do well and that they must remember these things and celebrate them. This can help them to feel confident and more ready to learn new skills.

I can do it

Focus

To help children to develop self-confidence and a willingness to try new things.

Activity

Ask the children to think of something they couldn't do a year or so ago, but which they can do now - e.g. ride a bike, swim, read a book, help in some way at home. All listen to children's oral responses.

I learned to swing myself on the playground swing.
It was hard at first.
I kept trying.
I watched
other people.
My dad helped me.
One day I found
I could do it.
I felt great.

Now ask the children to think about how they learned to do that thing. Ask them to close their eyes and concentrate on thinking back. Was it hard? Did they worry? Who helped them? How did they manage it in the end?

Ask children to tell you some of these things. Ask them to tell you how they felt when they could finally manage it.

Development

Talk about things they will be learning to do in the next class or school, or when they are grown up. Help them to understand that it will seem hard at first but that they will manage it, just as they managed other skills that they have already learned to do.

Ask children to think of one skill they have recently learned and to draw themselves learning to do it. Ask them to write about how they managed to learn to do it. Can they write down the steps to success?

(If your children have a book of achievement they can include this work.)

Reflection

Remind children that all adults had to learn many things before they were really grown up and that they may have felt unsure or worried at the time. Tell the children to keep remembering the things they are good at - this will give them confidence with new learning. Remind them that there are always people to help them.

At school I'm really good at...

I like making things, writing and drawing.
I like making things best.
This is me making a model of a car.

Focus

To help children to identify their own good personal qualities.

Activity

Talk with the children about their good qualities - reminding them of some of the things they told you in the last session. If you made a display, draw attention to it as a reminder. Ask the children to think about their own best quality. Ask them, for example if they are good at starting new work, good at getting on with it, good at finishing it, good at illustrating it. Are they good at maths, reading, creative work? Ask children to volunteer to stand up and say what they think they are good at. (You may need to help some of the more insecure children, and suggest something they are good at.)

Ask children to affirm what they are good at, by all standing up at once and whispering "I am really good at…"

Development

In PE or movement lessons ask the children to mime some of the things they are good at. You could ask half the class to do this while the other half watches and tries to guess what they are miming, before changing places to repeat the activity.

Ask the children to write down a list of three things they are really good at doing and to illustrate the one they like doing most.

We feel:
great,
super inside,
big, tall,
full of confidence,
happy,
on top of the world!

Reflection

Remind the children of the work they have been doing and tell them it is really important to be proud of what you can do well and that this confident feeling will help them when they are finding things not so easy. Remind them that we can't all be good at everything, but that we are all good at some things.

How do you feel about it?

Focus

To help the children to recognise when they have been successful, to know how to receive and give praise.

I felt really great when I got every one of my spellings right for the first time. I'm going to try to do this next week.

Activity

Ask the children to think about how they feel when they have done something really well - something that has turned out right. Ask them to give you some words to explain how they feel.

Ask the children how they know when they've done something to be proud of? Do they recognise this in themselves or do they rely on people to tell them they have done well? What do people actually say to praise their efforts? How do the children respond?

Development

Ask the children to think of how they look when they have done something really well. Ask them to draw a picture of themselves as they look and feel when they have done something really well.

Share their pictures and comments. Ask the children to try to capture and hold on to this feeling of being successful. Can they put it into words? Has it a colour or shape? Can they remember this feeling on occasions when they have not been successful at something? Can they recognise that they can't be successful at everything but they can always do their best - and this should help them to feel and look confident all the time.

Reflection

Remind the children that we all have different strengths and weaknesses. When they feel down about not doing something very well it helps if they can remember the times when they were successful. If people can remember this and try to do their best at all times they will feel more self-confident.

Let's celebrate!

On completion of these activities, don't forget to encourage children to evaluate their own learning by looking at what they thought or knew before doing the activities.

Bring together all the work the children have done in this set of activities in one large display. You could make it in five separate sections to correspond to the five activities.

Alternatively you can make the display as a whole class picture surrounded with some of the children's work. Ask the children to draw around two of them - a boy and a girl and use paint, collage or clothes to dress these two children. Give each child a speech bubble saying something such as "I know I can do it if I keep trying" or 'When I have practised a bit more I will be able to do it'. Surround the figures with children's work about how they

have practised a skill or how they have been determined to keep at their learning. Display other work from the children that you have gleaned from the activities, asking them to copy out pieces of work neatly for display. Ask the children to suggest titles for the display and to vote for the one they think is best.

Ask them to write about how they go about learning a new skill.

Share this display with the other classes in the school and invite parents and families to come and see the work.

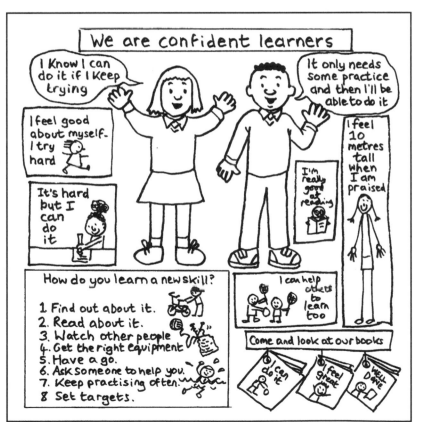

Look at relationships

Let's consider others, feel safe, trust, appreciate/value difference, recognise and challenge stereotypes.

Setting the scene for these activities

We all belong to various networks of families and friends. Children may need help in accepting and valuing contacts with people who are not their particular friends and who may move in different networks.

Picture storybooks about people/animals who are different will link with these activities. Choose those where the characters overcome obstacles or come to terms with the ways in which they are different. Books such as:

Something Else Kathryn Cave & Chris Riddell, Puffin
Dottie" Peta Coplans, Andersen
Elmer: the Story of a Patchwork Elephant David McKee, Red Fox
Oscar's Spots Janet Robertson, Blackie
Willy the Wimp Anthony Browne, Walker

The five activities in this section

What I like about you is…

This activity is to help children to identify positive qualities in people outside school and in their working group. You could further extend this by asking children to consider what they like about people in the media or characters in books. Then ask them each to make a list of three or four qualities - not physical skills - that they admire in people. Ask them to share their list with the rest of their working group and try to order this list in some way. Combine all the lists and order it. Invite the children - silently - to consider which of these qualities they value in themselves.

Caring

Children need help to think about support they give and receive. In this activity children are encouraged to visualise their feelings when helping someone and when someone helps them. You could extend this at the end of the session or day by asking each child to tell everyone of someone who has helped them that day and how they felt.

I'd like to be…

An activity to help children to recognise that everyone has good qualities - whether we like that person or not. As an extension activity you could ask children to think of a character they did not like in a book or on TV and to write what it is about this person that they don't like and to think of just one thing about the person that is likeable.

Underneath the surface

Children usually go by appearances and this activity asks children to look inside and underneath outward signs. You could further extend this activity by asking children to draw and write a story about someone who is different from them in some way - an alien, a foreigner, someone with a disability - but who has something about them that we would admire.

Be careful not to bully

Will the children in your class fall into the stereotype trap and think of a bully as someone different? Help children to realise that a bully is someone quite ordinary and often very nice who sometimes does things that can be thought of as bullying. Talk with the children about stories such as Red Riding Hood and people who are thought of as 'a wolf in sheep's clothing'. Remind the children of any stories you have recently read to them in which characters have exhibited bullying behaviour.

What I like about you is…

Focus

To help children to think about positive qualities in other people.

Activity

Ask children to sit in a loose group or circle and tell them to think about something they particularly like about someone in their family. You start by saying something about someone in your family e.g., "What I like about my brother is that he always cheers me up when I am sad."

Give everyone in the class the opportunity to say what they like about someone in their family.

Development

Ask children to focus on the children in the class and ask for volunteers to tell you all one thing they like about someone there. You could start this perhaps by finding something good to say about someone who is not always easy in class!

Ask children to write down something they like about each member of their working group - they could do this in a Zigzag book, draw each person and have a title page.

Children could write in their achievement books one or two of the positive statements other children in the class have made about them.

Shona
I like Shona because she is always cheerful and makes me feel happy. She always helps you if you are in trouble and never walks away.

Reflection

Remind children that it is easy to find something they like about people they like. It is harder to find something they can like in people who are not always very nice to them. Focusing on the good things about people helps us to relate to them in a more positive way and will help in forming good relationships.

Caring

Caring

In my picture I saw myself helping my friend to make a model. We worked together and it made me feel good to help him. My picture was orange and red.

helps glad super happy

Focus

To help children to visualise the support they can give to others and receive from them.

Activity

Ask the children to find a partner they know quite well and to sit down, hold hands, close their eyes and think of things they can do to help and support their partner. Ask them to try to make a picture of togetherness. Ask the children to tell you how they were feeling and what pictures came into their heads - what colours were in their pictures?

Then ask the children to draw a picture of their own face with their eyes closed and above their face to draw some of the things from the picture they made in their head. Can they write some of their feeling words around their picture?

Development

Ask the children to find a different partner, someone they don't know very well. This time ask them to make a picture in their head of this person helping them to do something they find hard to do.

Ask the children how they felt when someone they didn't know well was helping them. What sort of feelings did they have? What sort of picture did they make and what were the colours? Talk about helping all people - even people you may not know or like so well.

Ask children to draw a second picture - this time of someone helping them. Can they write some of their feelings around their picture? Ask if these were the same feelings as they wrote for their previous picture. You could display some of these pictures side by side or make two different displays.

Tell the children that people from other groups may also need our help and support - can they think of some? (e.g. people with special needs, in countries that need our aid, when tragedy strikes, in emergencies).

Reflection

Remind the children that we feel good when people help us and that we also feel good when we can help other people. Explain that it's easy to help our friends, but we can help people we don't know so well and this also makes us feel good.

I'd like to be...

Focus

To help children to recognise good qualities in other people.

Activity

Tell the children that there are some people that we like a lot, some that we don't like much and some that we don't know well enough to know if we like them or not. Tell them that we are all going to think of someone - not someone at school - we really like and why. You start by saying the name of someone you like, and why you like them. You can use TV personalities or someone you know - e.g. "I like Jake. He is a man who sells newspapers and always looks happy and cheerful." Ask children to volunteer to tell you about the person they have been thinking of.

Development

Ask children to close their eyes and think of someone else - perhaps of their own age, someone in their school, someone in their family, someone they have read about, a character in a book, etc. Ask the children to think of why they like this person. Make sure the children are telling you about personal qualities rather than looks.

Ask them to write down their reasons for liking this person on individual pieces of paper, cut them out in interesting shapes and place all these words on a large paper.

Ask the children if they can use all/some/a few of these words about themselves.

Look again at all the words they have written; there may be many duplicates. Count the duplicates, write the total on one and discard other copies of that word.

Select each word to mount on the paper to display and vote for a title. Encourage children to use these words as spelling checks or as stimulation for creative writing.

Reflection

Remind the children that there is something in everyone that makes people like them - but sometimes we have to look hard before we find it.

We like people who are..
cheerful, happy. friendly,
helpful, confident, supportive,
always there for you,
never miserable.

Some people always...
cheer you up,
listen to you,
play with you,
help you,
smile a lot.

Underneath the surface

Focus

To help the children to look beyond outward appearances when looking for values.

Activity

Before the lesson make up two parcels - one with something small, beautiful and valuable wrapped in plain paper, the other something valueless in glorious wrappings.

With the children around you in a close group, show them the two parcels. Ask them to tell you which they would rather have. Ask them to guess what might be in each. Take a vote on which to open first. Open the parcels and discuss the contents.

Explain to the children that people can be like these parcels - they might look dull on the outside but be really interesting and worthwhile on the inside. Similarly, people who look exciting and fun to be with might turn out to be not interesting- or bad friends.

Development

Ask the children to think of people they know - outside school - and to draw a picture of one who would make a good friend - even though they might not look so good on the outside. Ask the children not to name the person in their picture but to write around their picture all the things they think are good about this person.

Reflection

Remind the children that just as they are looking underneath the surface when thinking about other people, so other people will be looking underneath their surface! How do they measure up - are they the stuff of good relationships?

My friend is my Grandad. He is old and walks slowly but he likes to tell me stories about when my Dad was a little boy.

Be careful not to bully

Focus

To help children realise that a bully can be anyone and that anyone can be a bully. To help children to avoid the stereotype trap.

Activity

Ask the children to draw a picture of someone being bullied and then draw the person doing the bullying. Ask them to tell you/write down what is happening in their picture.

Ask the children to share their pictures with the whole group. Have any fallen into the stereotype trap and drawn the person doing the bullying as strong, big, fierce, ugly etc? Has anyone drawn someone who is none of these things?

Ask the children about some of the things that bullies do. Ask if they think they have ever done any of these things themselves without realising that it was bullying.

Development

Ask the children to look at their pictures again and to put themselves in the picture. What are they doing in the picture? What are they going to do?

Ask them to write down what they think they should do if they see bullying.

Now ask the children to look at the three people in their pictures again - is it easy to tell which is which?

Ask them if someone who takes things or someone who tells lies looks any different from the rest of us. As a class talk about the dangers of labelling people.

Reflection

Remind the children that it is what people do that makes them a bully, not what they look like - and that it is the same for all people. Normally, unless people wear special clothes or carry equipment for their work we can't tell what they are like just by looking at them. Remind children about the dangers of labelling people or discriminating against people who look different in some way. We need to look at the inner person - what they say and what they do - before making up our mind whether we want to be with them or not.

This is me watching someone bullying a friend.

The person bullying looks like anyone else but she is sometimes horrid and tries to make people do things that are not safe.

LEAVE HER ALONE!

I shall have to tell someone.

Let's celebrate!

On completion of these activities, don't forget to encourage children to evaluate their own learning by looking at what they thought or knew before doing the activities.

You could ask each child to draw her/himself at the centre of a network with their friends drawn around. The children could link their friends to themselves with threads to show a connection. They could include on their work the places where they usually meet these friends.

Evaluate the learning from the activities with the children by asking them to list what they think they knew beforehand and what they have learned. Ask them to write down anything they think they need to do or practise in order to improve their relationships with other people.

The five activities could form the basis of a year or class assembly in which children could select a piece of written work, drawing or painting to present. Older children could organise this themselves - putting themselves in groups to present the five different activities. For younger children you could ask each working group to take one activity to present. You might like to ask a good reader to read one of the stories from the list on page 78 or to tell the story in their own words.

Empathy and sympathy

Let's put ourselves in someone else's place - feel their feelings with sympathy and recognise their needs.

Setting the scene for these activities

Children need help to understand how other people feel and think - it is not easy for them to put themselves in someone else's place and think sympathetically of how the person might feel. These activities help children to think about other people, their qualities and their feelings, and to know how to act when people are feeling sad, lonely, clumsy, different.

Ask older children to define empathy and sympathy. Empathy here means to share someone's feelings with understanding and compassion, to identify with them. Sympathy means more or less the same - comforting, consoling, concerned about - rather than having pity for.

Look for picture books and stories that deal with loss, separation, jealousy - stories of people/animals who are different, have special needs or who show they are aware (or unaware) of other's feelings. Books such as:

Seal Surfer Michael Foreman, Andersen Press
Katie Morag and the Tiresome Ted Mairi Hedderwick, Picture Lions
Dogger Shirley Hughes, Picture Lions
John Brown, Rose and the Midnight Cat J. Wagner, Picture Puffin

The five activities in this section

Harry's shoes

Here children are asked to put themselves in someone else's place - to think of how Harry is feeling, to feel for him, to think of how they should act with sympathy and what they should say. You could extend this activity by asking children to put themselves in other people's places - someone who is ill, has a problem, finds things difficult. In other story reading you could ask the children how they would feel if they were one of the characters.

Someone different

This activity helps children to recognise that we are all people, however different we might be. Extend this activity by reading stories of people who are different in some way - perhaps stories of people who overcome disabilities or difficult situations. You will find *It's good to be different* a useful book (see Bibliography).

Jojo overdoes it

Children are always getting things wrong and how comforting for them to realise that they are not alone. The underlying theme of this is to accept other people's mistakes in a sympathetic, kindly and understanding way and not make things worse by unkind laughter. Extend this idea by taking about the need to 'have a go' even if you get things wrong or it turns out badly - because if we are not brave enough to try we would never do anything!

Dan all alone

An activity which helps children to realise that it is OK to talk about feelings to someone they know well. Many children (especially boys) find talking about their feelings difficult and they need the language and opportunity to do this. In your everyday classroom practice make a point of talking about feelings and asking children to tell you how they are feeling at times when things are good as well as bad.

Just as you are

In this activity children are asked to consider differences between people. To avoid emphasis of pupil differences talk about adults or story characters. You could extend the alien idea by asking children to tell the alien about other aspects of human behaviour - friendships, shyness, feelings, family life, sport, TV, music. Talk about how unfriendly and uncomfortable the world would be if people were not empathetic and sympathetic to one another.

Harry's shoes

Focus

To feel empathy and sympathy for someone who is feeling unhappy, and to think of ways to make the situation better.

I think Harry feels...
upset
worried
sad
unhappy
angry
anxious.

I think Harry...
is tired of looking
won't sleep
keeps thinking of Dodo.

Activity

Tell the children that you know a boy called Harry who is feeling very unhappy because his rabbit Dodo escaped from its hutch and is missing. Everyone in his family has been out looking for it but no-one can find it and they think it might be lost forever. Ask the children to think about how Harry is feeling.

Can they put themselves in Harry's shoes? Can they make their faces and bodies show what Harry might be feeling? What could they do and say to try to make Harry feel better, and to show that they understand Harry's feelings and feel for him?

Listen to and talk about responses from the children.

Development

Reflect on the various responses the children have made. What might be the best things to say and do? Are they just trying to cheer Harry up or can they realise that he needs time to be sad and to keep his good memories about Dodo safe? Ask the children to work in pairs or small groups to make a memory book about all the things Harry might have done with Dodo before it escaped. You could display the books under a heading such as "We tried to put ourselves in Harry's shoes."

Reflection

Help the children to understand that putting ourselves in 'someone else's shoes' can help us to understand how that person feels and this will strengthen the relationship. Remind children that this can be difficult, especially if the person is not of our group, culture, race etc.

Understanding and being able to appreciate and deal with another person's point of view is an essential skill for young people to master - it helps children to feel good about themselves when they can understand how others are feeling.

Someone different

Focus

To help the children to recognise that appearances can be deceptive.

Activity

Talk to the children about the differences between people. Remind them that some of these differences can be very small - twins have small differences - and some can be large - children with disabilities, different backgrounds, colour, religion and race.

Ask the children to draw a quick picture of someone who is different from themselves. Look at their pictures and talk about the differences. How in their pictures are the people different?

This is an opportunity to talk about differences between children in your class and also to look at the wider issue of discrimination.

Development

Ask the children to draw a child in a wheelchair. (NB If someone in your school needs a wheelchair ask them to draw someone with some other outward sign of a disability - who uses crutches, who cannot speak clearly, is deaf, blind or who has a disfigurement such as a birthmark etc.)

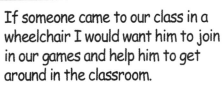

If someone came to our class in a wheelchair I would want him to join in our games and help him to get around in the classroom.

Ask the children to write down how they think this person would feel if they were in your class. What could the children do to make the child feel better about themselves? How could they help the person to understand that their 'difference' does not matter in your class? Help them to understand that the person doesn't really want our sympathy or pity - but wants to be accepted for what s/he is.

Reflection

Remind the children that people are all 'brothers under the skin' and that we have to accept people just as they are if we want to have a good relationship with them. We can't change how people look, but we can find out what they are really like before we decide whether we want to be their friends. Knowing how to deal with 'difference' in a positive way helps children to feel good about themselves.

Jojo overdoes it

Focus

To help the children to understand that sometimes people who make silly mistakes are really sorry and perhaps didn't mean them. We need to understand their mistakes and their feelings, forgive them and give them a second chance - making it easy for them to say they are sorry. Children may need help in not laughing at someone or allowing them to be dubbed 'a class clown'.

Activity

Tell the children about Jojo who was always getting things wrong. Jojo tried hard, but somehow things never turned out the way he wanted them to. If he watered the plants he would overdo it and water would pour out of the pot. If Jojo painted, he would put too much paint on and make a swirly grey wet mess. He didn't mean to get things wrong, but that is what happened. And everyone always laughed at him or said things like "Jojo's done it again."

Ask the children to suggest other things that Jojo might overdo.

How do the children think that Jojo might feel when people laughed at him?

Development

Ask the children to think of ways to help Jojo and what advice they would give to Jojo to try to get things right. Ask the children to write down their advice and to write down what they could do and say to make Jojo feel better about always getting things wrong.

Reflection

Remind the children that we all do things that turn out wrong sometimes and that it does not help when people make fun of us or laugh. We have to think about how other people are feeling when things go wrong for them - and make sure we do not make things worse by thoughtless comment or unkind laughter.

We think Jojo might feel:

sad, fed up,
cross with himself,
that he was no good,
unhappy when people
laughed at him.

Dan all alone

Dan feels:

sad,
lonely,
unhappy,
miserable,
cross,
fed up.

Focus

To help children think of other children's feelings, to extend their language of feelings so they can express their own feelings. To help children to realise that it helps to talk about their feelings to someone they can trust.

Activity

Tell the children this story:

"Dan's best friend went to live in another country. Dan felt sad at home and sad at school. He didn't want to play with other children. He just wanted his best friend back. One day the teacher asked Tim to sit next to Dan in his old friend's seat. This made Dan very sad and angry. He wouldn't talk to Tim and turned his book away to work alone."

Ask the children to think of how Dan was feeling. Can they give you words to describe this?

Ask children who offer words to write them on the chalkboard.

Ask the children to put themselves in Dan's place and think what they could do to remember his friend. Ask them to work in pairs to write a letter from Dan to his old friend.

Development

Ask the children to think of how Tim was feeling. What could he do to help Dan?

Ask the children to write a message from Tim telling Dan how he (Tim) was feeling.

Ask the children to suggest some things that children in Dan's class could do together to help Dan and Tim feel better.

Reflection

Remind the children that it is not always easy to help people who are feeling unhappy. Thinking of how they feel and understanding why they feel this way can help. Explain that it is important to talk about your feelings to someone you know well. If you do this, they can help you. Having the language to talk about your feelings is important - it helps you to feel good about yourself if you can explain how you feel.

Just as you are

We have drawn us with an alien from another planet. We are helping the alien to feel 'at home' on earth.

We'll help you

Focus

To help children to respond to the feelings of others - especially shyness and difference.

Activity

Ask the children to tell you what being shy really means. Come to agreement - and write a definition down. Ask the children to tell you how the shy person might feel and in what situations they would be shy and not shy.

Ask the children to close their eyes and think of a time when they were shy. How did it feel? What did they do? How could they help someone who is shy?

Ask the children to draw a picture of themselves helping a person who is shy. Can they write what they are doing and how the shy person feels now?

Development

Ask the children first to tell you how all children are the same. Then ask them to tell you how children are different. They will probably tell you about physical differences - eye and hair colour, for example. Focus on other differences - personality, ability, hobbies.

Ask the children to think of how people are different if they come from a different country, have different kinds of food, clothes, customs.

Ask the children how they themselves might feel if they were transported immediately to some other classroom in a different country.

Ask the children to think how someone from another planet might feel if they were transported to your classroom now. What could the children do and say to them to make them feel comfortable?

Ask them to work in pairs and draw a picture of themselves helping someone from a different planet to feel comfortable in your classroom. They can talk about this, plan their work, write about their picture and suggest ways of displaying their work.

Reflection

Remind the children that we are not all the same - we all have some differences and that we must learn to respect the ways in which other people are different. It is not enough to accept people who are different - we must try to make them feel part of our community.

Let's celebrate!

On completion of these activities, don't forget to encourage children to evaluate their own learning by looking at what they thought or knew before doing the activities.

To help the children to sum up the work they have done in this section you could ask each child to make a booklet with a decorated cover picture of a mechanical person or robot. Ask the children to use the four pages for:

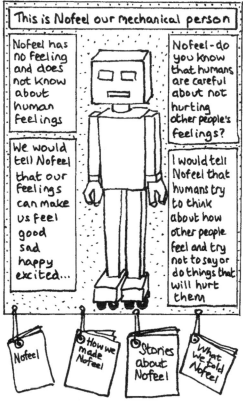

Page 1   Cover - a description of the robot - how it moves, talks, what it does.

Page 2   An explanation about how the robot has no feelings and cannot think for itself.

Page 3   The robot asking for information about human feelings.

Page 4   A picture of the author giving the robot information about how we try to think of how other people may be feeling, making sure we don't hurt their feelings and giving advice about the importance of talking about feelings.

The children could make a large robot and vote on the best name for it. During discussion children could agree on writing to add to their robot display, which could be presented in large writing via your computer. You could display some of the children's booklets around it and ask them all to write a letter telling the robot about thinking of other people's feelings.

Try, co-operate and succeed

Let's work together, share ideas, play our part, observe the rules, think about our responsibilities, feel good about our class and work.

Setting the scene for these activities

In this section children are helped to understand the rules, face up to their responsibilities and realise the need for co-operation at school and home. As children grow they can take increasingly more responsibility for their work in school and feel good about it when they have done well.

Look for picture storybooks where the characters have to co-operate in order to succeed or fit in with others, or where they have to join forces to overcome problems - books such as:

Timid Tim and the Cuggy Thief John Prater, Red Fox

It's Your turn Roger Susanna Gretz, Red Fox

Pumpkin Soup Helen Cooper, Doubleday

Farmer Duck Martin Wadell, Walker

The Patchwork Quilt Valerie Flournoy, Bodley Head

The Travelling Musicians P K Page, Viking

The Wild Washerwomen John Yeoman, Hamish Hamilton Ltd, Penguin

The five activities in this section

Our responsibilities

As children grow their responsibilities increase and this activity helps children to be proud of these new responsibilities. You could extend this activity by asking the children to make a "What I can do now" booklet or one about "What I look forward to being able to do." To increase children's involvement in their own learning you could ask them to decide how to sum up and present what they now think about their responsibilities.

Rules are OK!

This activity helps children to recognise the need for rules in society and to feel good about being able to obey them. Extend this learning by asking children to draw and write about what might happen if there were no rules. They could find out about who makes the rules in school/society.

I know I should but...

This scenario helps children to think about how they should act in everyday life but also how they can act in an emergency. You can extend the activity by talking about emergency procedures and first-aid - do any of the children know the recovery position and ABC - to check airways, breathing and circulation?

Let's find out together

Working together in pairs and groups can enhance self-esteem of children who need help in organising their work. They can feel proud of the end result even though their own input may have been small. Ask the children to tell you how they feel about working in this way and to identify what is good (and not so good) about it.

Classroom values

It is not easy for children to evaluate their own work - they tend to judge by quantity and neatness rather than content. Extend the activity by talking about this. Ask them to think about what they as individuals could do to improve their work and to write this up as a target.

Our responsibilities

Focus

To help the children to realise that they already have some responsibilities and that these will increase as they grow up.

Activity

Explain to the children that we have to keep our school a safe and healthy place. Tell them some of the things that grown-ups do to make sure this is so.

Ask the children to tell you all the things that they themselves do to keep the classroom a safe, healthy and happy place. Make a list of them.

Discuss responsibilities that older children have in your school - for example looking after the school environment, acting as a befriender or a peer supporter or playground mediator. Can the children see that in time they will be able to take on these responsibilities? Can they peer-teach now, in your class?

Development

Ask the children to think of things they do (or could do) at home to show they are a responsible person. Ask them to tell you what they can do and how much responsibility they can already take. Do they come to school, via a safe route, by themselves? Ask them to make pictures showing themselves doing some of the things they do for other people and things for which they are responsible.

> Oh yes
>
> We are responsible for:
>
> keeping the classroom tidy
> putting our work in the right place
> getting on with our work
> remembering what to do next
> putting paper towels in the bin
> putting waste paper in the bin
> keeping the scissors in a safe place
> clearing up after painting.

I am responsible for clearing the table after breakfast.

Reflection

Remind the children that when they were babies, someone else had to do everything for them. Now that they are growing up they can begin to learn to do some of these things for themselves, so that when they are grown-up they will be a thoughtful, sensible and responsible person. Children who can accept responsibility feel more in control and have greater self-esteem.

Rules are OK!

Some safety rules
Think first.
Keep your head.
Know the dangers.
Hold hands.

Focus

To help the children to understand why there are rules and why everyone needs to obey them.

Activity

Ask the children to tell you the classroom rules and briefly write these up. Talk about why these rules are necessary. What might happen if there were no rules? Ask the children to think of which rule is the most important - take a vote on this. Allocate a different area of the room for each rule and ask the children to go and stand by their rule. Ask older children to make a record of what they have done and what for the majority is the most important classroom rule. Do you agree with the children about the most important rule?

Development

Talk with the children about times when they have been out without an adult in charge of them. What were they doing? Where were they going? How did they feel about being out without supervision? What rules or warnings were they given by adults before they went?

Which are very specific rules - e.g. about crossing roads? Which were more general rules?

Can the class think up one rule which would work for them to keep them feeling safe and confident wherever they were going?

Ask older children to explore the following scenario:

You are with your friend, walking through the pathway/subway to the bus stop. A group of older people start to follow you and behave in a threatening way.

Does the one rule apply? Is there a need for a rule about finding help? Ask them to practise asking for help, giving accurate information, ways of staying calm under pressure.

Reflection

Remind the class that rules are there to help us, so that we know what to do to keep safe and confident. Rules tell us how to behave in various places pr situations so that everyone knows this. Explain that they need to know where they live, how to get home, who is there, how to contact them in an emergency, whom they could safely ask if they are in the town or some other place, how to use an emergency telephone. Children with these skills have good self-esteem.

I know I should, but...

Focus

To help the children to realise that we all have to exercise self-discipline, work together and think of the outcome to situations.

Activity

Tell the children about Ashley who found it difficult to do what he knew was right. (Change the name if you have an Ashley in your class.)

Ashley always wanted to play and didn't like to help. If his Mum asked him to lay the table, he was always busy doing something else. If Dad wanted him to help to clean the car or water the flowers, Ashley always had an excuse. One day his parents were very late home from the shops and Ashley was at home with his Gran, who had a poorly leg and couldn't walk much. Gran asked him to help her to get the things ready for tea but Ashley said that he was too busy playing. Gran tried to do it, but her leg gave way, she fell over and was hurt.

Ask the children how they thought Ashley felt and what they would like to say to him. Ask them how they think the story might end.

This is what really happened:

When Ashley saw what happened, he helped his Gran up to the chair and made sure she was comfortable. Then he dialled 999 and asked for the ambulance. When the ambulance people came they helped his Gran to bed. Then Ashley thought for a bit and began to tidy away his toys. He set the table for tea, and laid a tray for Gran so that when his parents came home they could take her something to eat in bed. He remembered that he mustn't put the kettle on, but he did fill it with water. As soon as his parents came in he told them what had happened. They were pleased that he had been so sensible.

Development

Ask the children to think of things they could do to show that they are growing up and can be more responsible. Do they take responsibility for anything at home? Ask them to write down the things they think they can do for themselves without people asking.

Reflection

Remind the children that as they grow they will have to think ahead, think of others and the outcome of their actions - and do things they should, even if they don't really want to.

Let's find out together

Focus

To help children understand the importance of co-operation and working together.

Activity

Ask the children to work in pairs or threes within their group and talk about things they each like and dislike. Ask them to decide on one thing they both like and both dislike, and who shall tell the rest of the group.

Ask the children to share their work with their group and try to agree on one thing they all like/dislike and who shall tell the class.

Come together as a class and ask one child from each group to stand up to tell what their group likes/dislikes.

Development

Ask each pair to co-operate in making a picture in two halves about their likes and dis-likes. Ask the children to write down what they did to help them to decide what to draw and how they organised this.

Reflection

Remind children that we all like and dislike different things, but there are usually things we have in common. We must respect other people's likes and dislikes.

Explain that working in this way - pairs/groups - helps us to co-operate and share ideas. Tell the children it is a useful skill to learn to 'work together and come to agreement' and helps them to feel confident about their work which make them feel good.

Classroom values

Focus

To help the children to value the people in their class and the work they themselves do well.

> We care about others in our class,
> share our things,
> don't interrupt,
> listen to what people say,
> behave sensibly,
> remeber the rules,
> help other people.

Activity

Ask the children to think of what they do at school that shows they care about all the other people in their classroom. Collect their responses and write these up somewhere where the children can see them.

Ask the children to choose and illustrate one of these responses.

Development

When the children have finished the above work, ask them to bring it with them and sit in a group with you. Ask them to look at their work and think whether this is their best work, not quite their best work, or not very good at all.

Ask them to tell you:

- how they feel when they know they have done good work
- how they can try to improve on work they have not done so well.

Ask them to devise a way of evaluating their work before they decide it is finished - e.g. a symbol to put alongside it to say it is their best work, or that they will try harder next time.

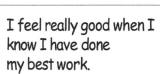

I feel really good when I know I have done my best work.

Yes!

Reflection

Remind the children that we need to show that we value the people in our class.

We also need to value our work. The best way to do this is to look at it carefully before we say it is finished - to be proud of it when it is really good - to know to try harder next time if it is not quite so good. Knowing when they have tried their best is a great boost to their self-esteem.

Let's celebrate!

On completion of these activities, don't forget to encourage children to evaluate their own learning by looking at what they thought or knew before doing the activities.

You could help the children to organise a class assembly to focus on achievements bringing together the work in these five activities.

There are several displays you could make with the children:
- What we are looking forward to being able to do.
- If there, no rules.
- Learn your ABC - about first-aid and secondary aid.
- We can work together - about ways the children enjoy doing this.

Ask the children to make badges to wear for various reasons for:
- sticking to the rules
- working well together
- being responsible
- reaching their own targets.

I made this badge – it is for reaching my target on learning spellings.

This is the school nurse. She came into school to help us learn about first aid and emergency procedure.

Bring it altogether

Before you leave this work altogether have a final winding-up session where you look at some of the successful things the children have done in the various sets of activities. Reflect on the assemblies, the displays, the work in their books and how they have shared this work with other children, other classes and their families and friends at home.

If you have done activities from all the ten sections, why not give the children a tick sheet that will allow them to reflect on and write about one thing they have learned from each section.

You might devise a letter to families similar to this one - ask children for their suggestions and encourage them to add their own comments on the other side.

Remind the children that as they grow they will be increasingly in charge of themselves and that it is up to them whether they feel good about themselves - or not.

They will have responsibilities that they can take upon themselves or have responsibilities thrust upon them. They have to decide whether to shoulder these responsibilities in a positive way and enjoy the growing up process - or not.

Explain that there will be times when their self-esteem is low and that this too is part of growing up - the trick is to remind ourselves of the things we can do and things we like doing and not let ourselves feel down-hearted. And finally, …

To celebrate completing all the activities why not:

- Award the children a certificate to take home to show their families They could devise their own or you could find a framework on your computer for the children to complete
- Celebrate in style with a celebration party with drinks and biscuits and invite the headteacher to present the certificates. This will be good for everyone's self-esteem.

Dear family,
We have been learning about feeling good about ourselves and improving self-esteem.

We made displays about...................
....
We invited people to talk about...........
....
I have learned that.................................
....
I know it is important to.........................
....
I have set myself a target to...................
....
love from ....

CERTIFICATE

This recognises that

Rashid

IS ALWAYS

thinking of others

By: Katee   Date: 1/4/01

CERTIFICATE OF FRIENDSHIP

Mary Ann

FROM

Janie

"I Did It Myself" Award

Presented to:

Roffie

By Mr Greentree

For Knowing my 5x table

Date May 3, 2001

Conclusion

Work on self-esteem is an ongoing process. As the children grow they will need ever more guidance of the way to go about things. Carrying out these activities and tasks is a way of opening a door towards a healthier aspect of personal and social wellbeing - but it is only a start. The ethos of your classroom and of the school is set by you and others and the children respond to this.

One way of child centred evaluation is to ask children what they know or think about each topic before you start, and then to ask them after completing the activities. Have they travelled a journey - and do they realise this?

At the end of the work you have done with the children, carry out your own personal evaluation of the ethos of your classroom. Ask yourself these ten questions - you can probably think of more!

1. Do the children feel good about themselves and confident to learn?
2. Have you found that the activities have made the children more thoughtful towards each other?
3. Are the children thinking before they speak?
4. Do they consider other people's feelings?
5. Have they a better vocabulary of feelings?
6. Are they more able to communicate - especially their feelings?
7. Are they more able to deal with pressures using relaxation and calming techniques?
8. Are the children more aware of their responsibilities and has this improved the climate in your classroom?
9. Do they understand that their behaviour leads to outcomes for which they are responsible?
10. Are they more able to work with their peers and is this collaborative work of a good standard?

If even a few of these questions have a positive answer, well done you!
Award yourself a very large gold star!
This will improve your self-esteem!

Well Done ME!

Synopsis of books used in the activities

Nothing

A little toy creature lies lost and forgotten in the attic. Removal men who come to take away the furniture see the old and battered toy and say "Oh it's nothing." The toy cannot remember anything about itself - not even its name and thinks that 'Nothing' must be its name. Nothing sets off on a journey of discovery to find out about itself. With the help of several animal characters Nothing eventually meets up with its original owner and finds out his real name before being mended, washed and lovingly accepted by a new generation in the family.

Mrs Spoon's Family

Mrs Spoon has a large dog as her family until a bedraggled cat turns up at the door one wintry night. Dog and Cat become great friends until they suffer jibes and mockery from cat neighbours on one side and dog neighbours on the other. These neighbours try to come between Mrs Spoon and her unorthodox family and almost succeed. Thankfully the strength of true friendship wins through in this important story about prejudice and stereotypes. The humorous illustrations add to the text and the children's enjoyment.

What Makes Me Happy

A picture book which illustrates many different feelings and emotions - such as what makes children laugh, cry, pleased, jealous, scared, excited, cross. A good book for sharing with children and using the illustrations to promote discussion about the various things that make them feel these, and other, emotions.

Amazing Grace

Grace wanted to act the part of Peter Pan in the school play but she is told that she cannot do this because Peter Pan is a boy. Grace thought she could overcome this and even the fact that Peter Pan wasn't black. She went to see the ballet, practised dancing and became even more determined to be Peter Pan. The class had to vote for the person to play this important part and all the children voted for her. This lovely story illustrates the importance in having determination of the face of all odds.

Full Story Book List

Amazing Grace, Mary Hoffman, Frances Lincoln. 1991
Badger's Bad Mood, Hiawyn Oram & Susan Varley, Picture lions. 1999
Badger's Bring-Something Party, Hiawyn Oram & Susan Varley, Andersen. 1994
Daisy Rabbit's Tree House, Penny Dale, Walker. 1997
Dogger, Shirley Hughes, Red Fox. 1998
Don't forget to Write, M Selway, Red Fox. 1993
Dottie, Peta Coplans, Andersen. 1993
Elmer: the Story of a Patchwork Elephant, David McKee, Red Fox. 1990
Farmer Duck, Martin Wadell, Walker. 1995
I love you Blue Kangaroo, E.C.Clark, Andersen, London. 1998
It's Your turn Roger, Susanna Gretz, Red Fox. 1996
Izzy and Skunk, Marie-Louise Fitzpatrick, David & Charles Children's Books London. 2000
John Brown, Rose and the Midnight Cat, J Wagner, Picture Puffin. 1979
Katie Morag and the Tiresome Ted, Mairi Hedderwick, Red Fox. 1999
Little Beaver and the Echo, Amy MacDonald, Walker Books, London. 1993
Mary Mary, Sarah Hayes & Helen Craig, Walker. 1992
Mrs Gaddy and the Ghost, Wilson Gage Bodley Head. 1981
Mrs Spoon's Family ,Malorie Blackman, Andersen Press. 1995
My Great Grandpa, Martin Waddell, Walker. 2001
Nancy No-Size, by Mary Hoffman and J Northway, Little Mammoth. 1990
Nothing, Mick Inkpen, Hodder. 1996
Omnibomulator, Dick King-Smith, Young Corgi. 1996
Orlando's little while friends, A Wood, Child's Play. 1981
Oscar got the blame, Tony Ross, Beaver. 1989
Oscar's Spots, Janet Robertson, Blackie. 1993
Piece of Cake, Jill Murphy, Walker. 1998
Pumpkin Soup, Helen Cooper, Picture Corgi. 1999
Ruby, Maggie Glen, Red Fox. 1992
Rumpelstiltskin, Helen Cresswell, Macdonald. 1998
Seal Surfer, Michael Foreman: Red Fox. 1998
Sheila Rae, The Brave, Kevin Henkes, Picture Puffins. 1990
Sing to the Stars, Mary B Barrett, Little, Brown & Co, Canada. 1994
Something Else, Kathryn Cave & Chris Riddell, Puffin. 1995
The Boy on the Beach, Niki Daly, Bloomsbury Publishing. 1999
The Nature of the Beast, Jan Carr, Tambourine Books. 1996
The Patchwork Quilt, Valerie Flournoy, Puffin. 1995
The Travelling Musicians, P K Page, Viking. 1992
The Wild Washerwomen, John Yeoman, Hamish Hamilton Ltd, /Penguin 1979
Timid Tim and the Cuggy Thief, John Prater Red Fox. 1994
Two Monsters, David McKee, Beaver. 1987

What else can you do?, Jean Marzollo Jerry Pinkney, Bodley Head. 1990
What makes me Happy?, Catherine and Laurence Anholt, Walker. 1992
Why is the sky blue, Sally Grindley & S Varley, Hodder. 1998
Wilfred Gordon McDonald Partridge, Mem Fox, Penguin. 1987
Willy the Wimp, Anthony Browne, Little Mammoth. 1990
Windhover, Alan Brown & Christian Birmingham, Collins. 1998

Bibliography:

Curriculum Guidance 5 - Health Education. National Curriculum Council,- out of print but copies in many schools.
The National Curriculum Handbook - for primary schools. Qualifications and Curriculum Authority. 1999.
Circle Time for the Very Young. M. Collins. Lucky Duck Publishing. 2001.
Picture This - Guided Imagery. Murray White. Lucky Duck Publishing Ltd. (CD, tape and booklet) 1999.
It's good to be different - Stories from the Circle. Neva Milicic. Lucky Duck Publishing Ltd. 1994.
Keeping Safe - safety education for young children. M Collins. Forbes Publishing Ltd. 1995.
Keep Yourself Safe - an activity based resource for primary schools. M Collins. Lucky Duck Publishing Ltd. 1997.
Let's get it Right for Nursery Children. M Collins. Forbes Publications. 1998.
Ourselves Resource Pack (Watch) N Wetton & M Collins. BBC Educational Publishing. 1998.
Birth, Care and Growth Resource Pack (Watch) N Wetton & M Collins. BBC Educational Publishing. 1999.
Celebrations - George Robinson and Barbara Maines. Lucky Duck Publishing Ltd. 1994

Margaret Collins is a teacher and former headteacher in infant/first schools. She is now Visiting Fellow at the Health Education Unit, Research and Development School of Education at the University of Southampton. She writes and co-writes teaching materials for children, books and articles on health education.